Famous American Belles
of the
Nineteenth Century

Famous American Belles of the Nineteenth Century

By

Virginia Tatnall Peacock

ILLUSTRATED

Philadelphia & London
J. B. Lippincott Company
1901

ELECTROTYPED AND PRINTED BY J. B. LIPPINCOTT COMPANY, PHILADELPHIA, U.S.A.

To

My Dear Mother

from whom I derived my first

conception of all that is

most beautiful in

woman

PREFACE

DURING the century now drawing to its close there have appeared in America from time to time women of so pre-eminent a beauty, so dazzling a wit, so powerful a magnetism, that their names belong no less to the history of their country than those of the men whose genius has raised it to the rank it holds to-day among the nations of the earth. Among them have been women of the highest type of mental and moral development, women of great political and of great social genius, all of whom have left the impress of their remarkable personalities upon their time. When they have manifested these qualities in their girlhood they have risen frequently to an eminence such as it is scarcely possible for the women of any other country to attain at a correspondingly early age.

From among the latter class the subjects of these sketches have been taken, those having been selected who seemed most adequately to represent their period and locality and whose fame was beyond question, it having been frequently of national and sometimes of international extent.

Rising to wield the magic of their influence in every

PREFACE

decade of the century and in every section of the country, some study of the time in which each lived has been necessary in order to give her her proper setting and to justly estimate the power she exercised.

The inventions and discoveries America has given to the world in this great century have made vast changes in our material condition, which, in turn, have been productive of striking contrasts between the existence of the women who gave life and color to the early years of the century and that of those who reflect the myriad advantages of its closing days.

It argues the possession of extraordinary attributes to have been a belle of wide repute in the days when there was no telegraph to flash the record of a woman's beauty, charm, or social progress from one end of the country to the other, when the press contained only the briefest accounts of purely local and wholly public events, when every letter that might or might not have contained her name or have been a herald of her loveliness cost its sender twenty-five cents a sheet in postage, when her few and simple toilets were painstakingly made by hand, when she went to balls on horseback, arriving sometimes with a wrinkled gown but seldom with a ruffled temper, when all travelling was done by means of a stage-coach, and a journey from one city to another was sometimes the event of a lifetime, and when the comparatively few women who crossed the seas did so in merchant vessels not infrequently owned by their own fathers, and spent many long weeks in the passage.

PREFACE

Those who come within the radius of its charm, however, easily recognize the power of a queenly personality, as the lives of the most illustrious men in every period of our history have borne testimony. Among the women who unite the centuries there is a brilliant promise, moreover, that there will be those in the twentieth, as there have been throughout the nineteenth, " to perpetuate that empire which beauty first established."

The writer gratefully acknowledges her indebtedness to all those whose courtesy or assistance has in any way lightened the task of collecting the data for these sketches; to those who by kindly lending portraits in their possession, as well as to those who by graciously permitting the use of their own portraits, have thereby added so much to the value and interest of this volume.

PARIS, June 22, 1900.

CONTENTS

LIST OF ILLUSTRATIONS

❦

LIST OF ILLUSTRATIONS

LIST OF ILLUSTRATIONS

MARCIA BURNS

(MRS. JOHN PETER VAN NESS)

ARCIA BURNS! What memories the quaint
Scotch lassie's name calls up!

The city of Washington disappears and its
site spreads before us in flourishing farm lands and
orchards. Scattered farm-houses raise their chimneys
amid primeval oaks and elms, and from the low door-
way of the humblest emerges the winsome form of
Marcia Burns. Six hundred acres, representing the
thrift of generations of Scotch ancestors, surround her.
The Potomac, one of the great water-ways of the
South, carrying the produce of the fertile lands above
into Alexandria for consumption or reshipment, almost
kisses her feet. This is her patrimony, over which
she has already heard such spirited debate between
her father and General Washington, then President of the United States, and the three gentlemen
commissioned by Congress, at that time sitting in
Philadelphia, to select and purchase the ground on
which is to be built the capital city. As she looks
riverward a canoe is beached in the shadow of the vine-
hung trees, and the President, accompanied by two of
the commissioners, whose forms have of late grown

familiar to her childish eyes, have come again to confer with her father, whom Washington has already dubbed "the obstinate Mr. Burns."

"And I suppose you think," says Burns, as the dispute again waxes warm, "that people here are going to take every grist that comes from you as pure grain. But what would you have been if you had not married the widow Custis?" Gracefully or ungracefully, however, he must eventually yield, for the "Widow's Mite," as Burns's acres were described in the land patent of 1681 which bestowed them upon his emigrant ancestor, form part of the tract which Maryland has ceded to the nation for its capital. Here is stalwart Johnson, governor of the State, to emphasize the fact with many a round oath that makes the gentle Marcia's heart stand still.

"And yonder lassie," says Daniel Carroll, "will be the greatest heiress hereabouts." Davy Burns' eyes wander towards his daughter. He is long silent. The shadows have lengthened into darkness when he says, "Very well, sirs, take the land, and I leave it to your fairness to fix the terms."

Supper is served, and the guests are accommodated for the night beneath the moss-grown roof of the attic, for Burns' cottage boasts but four rooms,—two sleeping-rooms, a sitting-room, and a dining-room, the kitchen being built apart from the house, as was the custom of the time and country. Unpretentious as the little abode is, the deed conveying the property to the commissioners, in trust for the government, provides

Marcia Burns
(Mrs. John Peter Van Ness)
From miniature by James Peale, 1797

that the streets of the new city shall be so laid out as not to interfere with it.

Marcia Burns was but yet a child when fate wrought the change in her destiny which no wisdom could have foreseen. By the death of her only brother she became sole heiress to what was at that time an immense fortune. Yet it is not through the magnitude of her wealth that she illumines the period in which the lines of her life were cast. It is through the exquisite qualities of a most exalted womanhood.

With wise forethought and some premonition of the change about to take place in her life, her parents placed her in the family of Luther Martin, in Baltimore. Martin was at that time at the height of his fame as an advocate at the Maryland bar. In the enlightened atmosphere of his home, Marcia grew up in close companionship with his daughters, her refined nature imperceptibly acquiring that ease and grace which were ever afterwards characteristic of her, and her receptive mind readily cultivating those attributes that were to render her most attractive in conversation to such men as Hamilton, Burr, Marshall, Randolph, and Webster.

That face of nature familiar to her from her infancy was in a state of unlovely transition when she again returned to her home. Verdant orchards and sloping meadow lands had been divided into building lots and crossed and recrossed by muddy thoroughfares. In what had been a piece of woods within a stone's throw of her father's home, the President's house was nearing completion. A mile and a half to the east, on the summit of a hill, the white walls of the Capitol were becoming visible to all the surrounding country. At irregular intervals houses, single and in rows, were in course of construction. There was nothing in the so-called city of Washington to which Marcia Burns came home, and of which the government took formal possession in 1800, that ever so remotely suggested the garden spot that it is to-day. Members of Congress and foreign ministers alike reviled it, and the lamentations of Mrs. Adams are too well known to be repeated here.

Of such social life as there was scattered over so vast an area of mud, in which "pedestrians frequently slumped and horses became stalled," Marcia Burns became a central figure. Though she was too gentle and modest ever to assume a leadership, yet all that was best and brightest in the life about her naturally gravitated in her direction.

Notwithstanding the pretentious homes that were going up around her, she still dwelt contentedly in her cottage of four rooms. There, in the summer evenings, gathered on the low, broad stone slab of its south door, overhung with blooming wistaria, her friends and neighbors,—the Tayloes from the afterwards famous Octagon house, the Calverts, and the Daniel Carrolls from Duddington Manor over near the Capitol.

In the winter season, when Congress was in session,

the cheery sitting-room and the hospitable dining-room were seldom without their guests. There came Aaron Burr, to flatter her as he flattered every attractive woman with whom he came in contact, and gallant Hamilton, the lover of all lovely women, and Randolph of Roanoke, seeking balm for his tempestuous spirit in that sweet and gracious presence, and Jefferson, to admire, with all the ardor of his democratic soul, the simplicity of her life. There, too, Tom Moore was entertained during his visit to Washington, whence he returned home to write things that did not make pleasant reading matter about the city and Mr. Jefferson, who was our President at the time and who had looked rather patronizingly upon the foppish little Irish bard. There also came suitors for the hand of Marcia, men with a nobility of soul that enabled them properly to estimate the beauty of her character, as well as men who were attracted simply by the stories of her great wealth.

In 1802, when she was twenty years old, she became the wife of John Peter Van Ness, a member of Congress from New York. He had been graduated from Columbia College and admitted to the bar of his native State. In 1800, when he was thirty years old, he was elected to Congress. His youth, his graceful, winning manners, his handsome countenance, and his wealth won him an easy popularity in the society of the capital.

Shortly after the death of Marcia's father, Van Ness erected, close by the old cottage, one of the handsomest houses of that day in the city and one that compares not unfavorably with the most elegant homes built there in recent years. It was designed and built by Latrobe at a cost of nearly sixty thousand dollars, its marble mantel-pieces, which are works of art, being imported from Italy. It had, moreover, a *porte cochère*, which was a rarity in those days,—the President's house having the only other one in Washington. A truly magnificent home it was, and destined to be the scene of many brilliant occasions, as also to witness days as full of heart-rending unhappiness to Marcia Burns as those both in the cottage of her girlhood and the home of her early married life had been of pure joyousness.

With all its treasures of art, the chief ornament of the new home was Ann Van Ness, who completed her studies at a boarding-school in Philadelphia and returned to Washington about the time her parents took possession of it. Two years later she married Arthur Middleton, of South Carolina, the son of a signer of the Declaration of Independence, and probably that same Arthur Middleton, of whom Mrs. Edward Livingston made mention in a letter to her husband ten years later to the effect that his moustaches, whiskers, and velvet shirt were creating more of a sensation in New York than the quarrel between Jackson and Calhoun. Ann died within a year after her marriage. She was an only child, and to her mother life held nothing that could amend her loss. Thenceforth she withdrew from the sphere to which she had been since her early girlhood so great an ornament. She frequently sought the seclusion of the little cottage, and there, perhaps, lived over in memory the days that had known no shadow.

She did not need the discipline of sorrow, which some natures require to sweeten them, but under its influence she rose to the loftiest heights of benevolence. Her pictured face reveals to us the beauty of her soul. The truth that speaks in her eyes, the spirituality of her brow, the tenderness of her mouth, combine to make the perfection of human character. The Washington City Orphan Asylum, which she founded and to which she devoted both time and means, is a fitting monument to her memory.

She died on the 9th of September, 1832, and is the only woman who was ever honored with a public funeral in Washington. Through her charities she had become as widely known and as tenderly loved in the later years of her life as she had been in her youth through qualities not less endearing.

The following tribute to her is by Horatio Greenough :

> "'Mid rank and wealth and worldly pride,
> From every snare she turned aside.
> She sought the low, the humble shed,
> Where gaunt disease and famine tread ;
> And from that time, in youthful pride,
> She stood Van Ness's blooming bride,
> No day her blameless head o'er past
> But saw her dearer than the last."

THEODOSIA BURR

(MRS. JOSEPH ALSTON)

THEODOSIA BURR was, as has been said of the daughter of another eminent statesman with whom Aaron Burr was closely identified, "the soul of her father's soul." If we would know the better part of a man who was one of the most remarkable characters of his age, we must know Theodosia, through whom, perhaps, his name, which all the subtlety of his soul was bent on immortalizing, may live to a better fame in the centuries to come than has attended it through the years of that in which he lived. Under the inspiration of her presence both her father and husband rose to lofty pinnacles in the political arena of their country. Her father on the eve of her marriage stood at the very portals of the Chief Magistracy. In less than ten years of political life he had so progressed that the election of 1800 resulted in a tie vote for the Presidency between Aaron Burr and Thomas Jefferson.

In 1801, while the festivities attending Theodosia's marriage at Albany were at their height, the House of Representatives at Washington entered upon that long session of seven days which terminated in declaring

THEODOSIA BURR

Thomas Jefferson President of the United States and Aaron Burr Vice-President.

From the moment Theodosia linked her life with another's, and thus in a measure ceased to be part of his, the retrogressive period of Aaron Burr's life began.

To her husband she carried that same inspiring influence which she had wielded over her father. She gave an impetus to his luxuriant and aimless existence, and at the time of the tragedy which ended her twenty-nine years of life he was occupying the gubernatorial chair of his State. Her life was closely allied not only with the private interests, but with the political ambitions of both. Her father rarely dined, either among friends or strangers, that her health was not drunk. He made her known to everybody, and during his travels in Europe so interested Jeremy Bentham and other writers in her that they sent her sets of their books.

At a time when woman was regarded rather as the companion of a man's heart than as his intellectual mate, " the soft green of the soul on which we rest our eyes that are fatigued with beholding more glaring objects," Theodosia Burr's mental faculties were so developed and trained as to fit her for the most complete and sympathetic union with father, husband, and son.

It is but a negative tribute to say that she was by far the best-educated woman of her time and country. In the beauty of her mind and person she realized her father's ideal of a perfect woman, and amply satisfied his pride and vanity. On the eve of his duel with Hamilton he wrote to her, "I am indebted to you, my dearest Theodosia, for a very great portion of the happiness which I have enjoyed in this life. You have completely satisfied all that my heart and affections had hoped for or ever wished."

Theodosia was the only child of Burr's marriage with the widow of a British army officer who had lost his life in the West Indies.

Fresh from the battle-fields of the Revolution, where he had won honors of which he was ever more tenacious than of those achieved elsewhere, and but recently admitted to the bar after a brief period of study, his marriage to a woman ten years his senior and the mother of two well-grown boys was a source of genuine wonderment to Burr's friends in New York. Young, of fascinating manner and appearance, some means, and good family, he might readily have aspired to an alliance with any one of those families which were a power in the State,—the Livingstons, the Van Rensselaers, or the Clintons. But before he quitted the army, Burr had discovered the charms of the society at the "Hermitage," presided over by Mrs. De Visme and her two daughters, one of whom was the widow of Colonel Prevost.

There he met the most distinguished men of his country, through whose influence this family had been spared the inconvenience of moving within the British lines at the outbreak of hostilities. In the library, there, he discovered a treasure-house of French literature, to which he was ever partial, and in the inter-change of thought which followed his reading, Aaron Burr and Mrs. Prevost became constantly more imbued with a sense of the beauty and attraction of each other's minds. Through her he gleaned his first reverence for the intellectual power of woman, and to her he owed the happiest days of his life.

" The mother of my Theo," he said, speaking of her towards the close of his life, " was the best woman and the finest lady I have ever known." In her finished manner, her fine bearing, and her exquisite mind there was a delicate harmony that soothed and satisfied Burr's artistic soul. His marriage to her in July, 1782, put an end to the rumor that he was paying his addresses to Miss De Visme, to which his frequent visits to the " Hermitage" had given rise.

The first year of their married life was spent in Albany, where he was engaged in the practice of law, and where Theodosia was born on the 23d of June, 1783. In the fall of that year her parents removed to the city of New York, where they had leased a house in Maiden Lane, at a rental of two hundred pounds per year, to commence from the time the British troops left New York, which they did on November 23, 1783.

So prosperous were Burr's financial affairs that he early in his married life acquired also the possession of a country seat, Richmond Hill, then two miles from the city. The house, a stately frame building with a lofty portico supported by Ionic columns, stood on a noble hill, several hundred feet in height, overlooking the river and the Jersey shore. It was surrounded by a lawn shaded by oaks, lindens, and cedars, on the outskirts of which on all sides stretched woods of more than a hundred acres. Within the enclosure was a pond known for many years after the property had passed from Burr's possession as Burr's Pond. On it Theodosia learned the graceful art of skating when still quite a little girl.

The house, built about the middle of the last century, was Washington's head-quarters in 1776, and Burr, who was there with him, conceived his first desire to become its possessor. It was occupied by John Adams during his tenure of the Vice-Presidency, when New York was the capital, and Burr's long possession of it culminated in the elegant hospitality of which it was the scene during his term as Vice-President. He returned there from Washington at the close of the sessions of Congress, and entertained with a lavishness that eventually bankrupted him.

His library, which bespoke the critical taste of the scholar, and which he had begun to collect as a boy, was a feature of the house, recalled in after years by men who had been his guests as vividly as the brilliant dinner parties given beneath the same roof by the distinguished Adams and his wife. He had his London bookseller, through whom he made constant additions to his collection, for Burr was ever a lover of books, and he recorded in his journal in his days of exile and want with what pangs he had been obliged to part with

Theodosia Burr
(Mrs. Joseph Alston)
By Charles B. J. F. Saint Memin

some odd volumes he had with him upon discovering that he was again under the necessity of dining.

His passion for books he imparted to his daughter, urging upon her at all times the necessity for study and improvement, and never relinquishing his endeavors to carry her mind to a high order of cultivation. In the communication he addressed to his son-in-law on the night before his duel with Hamilton, he asked as a last favor that he would urge Theodosia to continue to study. In all his letters to her his efforts to stimulate this habit were uppermost. " The longer I live," she wrote to him after her marriage, " the more frequently the truth of your advice evinces itself, that occupation is necessary to give us command over ourselves."

In the development of her mind and character he pursued a clearly-defined and well-directed course. When she was ten years old he wrote to his wife from Philadelphia, where he was at the time occupying a seat in the Senate, reminding her that he had left a memorandum of what Theodosia was to learn during his absence. While his public duties were such that he was not able always to personally superintend her studies, he gave minute instructions to the tutors to whom he intrusted her, and constituted himself their vigilant and inexorable critic. "If your young teacher," he wrote to her when she was in her sixteenth year, " after a week's trial should not suit you, dismiss him on any pretence, without wounding his pride, and take the old Scotchman. Resolve to succeed, and you cannot fail."

Mary Wollstonecraft's book, "A Vindication of the Rights of Women," in which Burr became so absorbed that he sat up all night reading it, so affected him that its influence told on all Theodosia's life. On the principles it inculcated were based both her mental and moral development. "If I could foresee," he wrote to his wife, "that Theodosia would become a mere fashionable woman with all the attendant frivolity and vacuity of mind, adorned with whatever grace and allurement, I would earnestly pray God to take her forthwith hence. But I yet hope by her to convince the world what neither sex appears to believe,—that women have souls."

"And do you regret," he wrote to Theodosia herself, when she was a little more than sixteen, "you are not also a woman? That you are not numbered in that galaxy of beauty which adorns an assembly-room? Coquetting for admiration and attracting flattery? No. I answer with confidence. You feel that you are maturing for solid friendship. The friends you gain you will never lose; and no one, I think, will dare to insult your understanding by such compliments as are most graciously received by too many of your sex."

Burr was himself an ornament to many a drawing-room, and no man ever had better opportunities for estimating the deficiencies in the system of educating the women of his day. Theodosia he brought up like a young Spartan, with few or none of the feminine affectations then in vogue. Courage and fortitude were his darling virtues, and so instilled into her from her infancy that they formed almost the groundwork of her character. "No apologies or explanations. I hate them," he said, reproving her for some fault of omission when she was a little child. "I beg and expect it of you," he wrote to her from Richmond, where he was awaiting trial for treason, and whither she was hastening to him, "that you will conduct yourself as becomes my daughter, and that you manifest no signs of weakness or alarm."

Theodosia's affection for her father was the absorbing passion of her life. "You appear to me so superior, so elevated above other men," she once wrote to him, "I contemplate you with such a strange mixture of humility, admiration, reverence, love, and pride, that very little superstition would be necessary to make me worship you as a superior being; such enthusiasm does your character excite in me. When I afterwards revert to myself, how insignificant do my best qualities appear. My vanity would be greater if I had not been placed so near you; and yet my pride is our relationship. I had rather not live than not be the daughter of such a man."

He sent his love to "the smiling little girl," in a letter he wrote his wife when Theodosia was two years old, not knowing that with his going she had not only ceased to smile, but that she wept bitterly and heartbrokenly whenever his name was mentioned, and that it required the combined efforts of her mother and nurse to divert her thoughts from the painful fact of his absence. As her mother said, the attachment which thus early manifested itself in so marked a manner, was not of a common nature. Theodosia's life is an evidence of how exalted it was, when, with all the world against him, she was yet proud to be his daughter.

Burr exercised an almost hypnotic influence over both men and women, and there are extant innumerable anecdotes of the conquests he continually made over those who had gone forth to apprehend him as a villain. In his intercourse with Theodosia he brought into play all those delicate attributes of his mind which captivated so many women. She was constantly in his thoughts. "The ideas of which you are the object, that daily pass through my mind," he wrote to her in 1799, from Albany, where the Legislature was in session, "would, if committed to writing, fill an octavo volume. . . . Indeed, my dear Theodosia, I have many, many moments of solicitude about you."

He exacted much of her even as a child, among other things that she should keep a journal in his absence, to be sent to him at regular intervals, and that she should answer his letters minutely and promptly. Writing to her when she was eleven years old, he said,—

"Yesterday I received your letter and journal to the 13th inclusive. On the 13th you say you got nine pages in Lucian. It was, to be sure, a most surprising lesson. I suspect it must have been the second time going over, and even then it would have been great, and, at the same rate, you will be through a second time before my month is up. I should be delighted to find it so. I have not told you directly that I should stay longer than a month but I was angry enough with you to stay three months when you neglected to write to me for two successive posts."

"I beg, Miss Prissy," he wrote to her from Philadelphia during the same year, "that you will name a single '*unsuccessful effort*' which you have made to please me. As to the letters and journal which you did write, surely you have reason abundant to believe that they gave me pleasure; and how the deuce I am to be pleased with those you *did not* write, and how an omission to write can be called an effort, remains for your ingenuity to disclose."

In his next letter to her, he referred again to "the unsuccessful effort."

"Your letter of the 9th, my dear Theo, was a most agreeable surprise to me. I had not dared even to hope for one until to-morrow. In one instance, at least, an attempt to please me has not been '*unsuccessful.*' You see, I do not forget that piece of impudence."

He was mindful, too, of her health, and in one of his letters begged her to carry herself erect. He had himself a remarkably erect and graceful carriage, which lent a majesty to his bearing and gave the impression of much greater height than he possessed.

While his letters to her were full of advice and suggestions for her improvement, they were by no means lacking in commendation. As she grew to womanhood this was more marked, as was also his tendency to confide in her. Her father's frequent and prolonged absences from home, her mother's long illness, attended with much suffering and terminating in death when Theodosia was but eleven years old, had necessitated an early assumption of those responsibilities which mature and strengthen character. To a suggestion contained in a letter written by her father shortly before her mother's death, that he would leave Congress that he might have more time to devote to his wife, Theodosia replied with a quaintness that was characteristic of her: " Ma begs that you omit the thought of leaving Congress."

From her close association with her mother under such circumstances her receptive mind became imbued with the beauties of the Christian philosophy, which her father, though a grandson of Jonathan Edwards and a son of the Rev. Aaron Burr, founder and first president of Princeton College, had not included in the course of studies so exactingly marked out for her. She was at this time studying Latin, Greek, French, and music, and learning to dance and to skate.

After her mother's death, Burr, who had a profound admiration for the language, literature, and people of France, consigned her to a French governess. She acquired a complete mastery of that tongue, and the fluency with which she spoke it added much to the grace with which she presided over her father's home, for Burr frequently entertained Frenchmen. Louis Philippe, Jerome Bonaparte, Talleyrand, and Volney were all at various times his guests at Richmond Hill.

When Theodosia was fourteen she took her place at the head of her father's household and became his inseparable companion, her playful wit illuminating his hours of relaxation, her steadfast courage, her strength, her very presence, constituting his most powerful defence in the darkest hours of his life.

She had much of her mother's self-poise and elegance of manner, together with her father's dignity and wit. When she reached maturity, though short in stature like her father's family, she carried herself with a noble dignity which, with a certain lofty benevolence of countenance, the refinement of her features, the frank intelligence of her brow, the healthful bloom of her complexion, made her singularly beautiful. So absolute was her father's confidence in her that he wrote when she was but seventeen, " Many are surprised that I could repose in you so great a trust as that of yourself, but I knew you were equal to it, and I am not deceived."

He sent Brant, the Indian chief, to her from Philadelphia with a letter of introduction,—she was but fourteen at the time and mistress of Richmond Hill, where she entertained him with an ease which gave her father much gratification. She gave a dinner in his honor, inviting to meet him some of her father's friends, among them Volney, Bishop Moore, Dr. Bard, and Dr. Hosack. She was already a belle, with many admirers ever in her wake, when Edward Livingston, then mayor of New York, taking her aboard a French frigate lying in the harbor of the city, thus warned her: " You must bring none of your sparks on board, Theodosia. We have a magazine here, and we shall all be blown up."

Her life was full of happiness at this time, with Hamilton's wife and daughters among her friends, her father one of the Presidential possibilities, and she enjoying much of his society, accompanying him frequently to Albany on horseback and visiting in the neighborhood while he transacted his business at the capital.

In February, 1801, a few months before she was eighteen, Theodosia was married to Joseph Alston, of South Carolina. He also was young, being but twenty-two, and wealthy, possessing extensive rice plantations, talented and ambitious, though as yet without a specific object on which to expend these qualities. He had studied law and been admitted to the bar, though he had not begun to practise. Upon Burr's suggestion he entered upon a political career, rising eventually to the governorship of his State.

Theodosia argued for a deferment of the marriage, quoting Aristotle, that a man should not marry till he was thirty-six. With convincing eloquence and ardor, Alston replied, winning his suit, notwithstanding Aristotle and other equally eminent authorities.

On February 7, 1801, the New York *Commercial Advertiser* announced the marriage, which had taken place on the 2d, at Albany, where the Legislature, of which Burr was then a member, was in session. It was a period of intense excitement throughout the country, and the names of Jefferson and Burr were in all mouths. The people of the country had cast a tie vote, which threw the election into the House of Representatives. Party spirit manifested itself for the first time in the young republic, and the strength of the constitution was early put to a severe test.

Theodosia, on her way to her new home in the South, stopped in Washington, where, on the 4th of March, she saw her father inducted into the Vice-Presidency.

Her marriage and her father's new honors inaugurated for her three years of absolute happiness. Though her husband's home and her father's were a journey of twenty days apart, she went frequently back and forth, and though she wrote to her husband during one of her early visits to her old home, "Where you are, there is my country, and in you are centred all my wishes," she was undoubtedly in better health and spirits when in her northern home. Her winters were passed in Charleston, where she was well received and much beloved, and where she became an important factor in her husband's political success.

Her father missed her sadly. "For what else, for whom else, do I live?" he had written to her shortly before her marriage. When she was no longer at Richmond Hill he returned there with painful reluctance. Theodosia urged him to marry again, and from the tone of a letter he wrote to her about this time there seems to have been some probability of his accepting her suggestion. If he were really in earnest, however, he at least did not conduct the affair with his usual sapiency, and though Theodosia from afar threw light on the young woman's vagaries, it was to no purpose.

Theodosia's only child, a son, she named after her father, to whom he was a source of much pride and affection. To Burr the anniversaries of the day of Theodosia's birth were ever occasions for rejoicing. Her twenty-first birthday, though she was not with him, he celebrated with a dinner-party at Richmond Hill. He had her portrait placed in a chair at the table, but, as it was a profile and appeared unsociable, he had it hung up again. "We laughed an hour, danced an hour, and drank your health," he wrote to her.

But already the days of her contentment were drawing to a close. Before this letter telling her of the happiness the day had given him had reached her, the tradegy of Weehawken had been enacted. Its shadow fell forever upon him who survived it, and who doubtless became a potent instrument in Hamilton's canonization. With awful blackness, too, it fell upon the far-away daughter when she heard that her father was a fugitive with an indictment for murder hanging over him.

From that moment shadows gathered about her with ever-increasing sombreness till they culminated in that hour of darkness in which her life went out.

In Burr's Mexican scheme, which he set on foot

shortly after the expiration of his term as Vice-President, Theodosia became involved sentimentally, and her husband financially. The President's proclamation and Burr's arrest put an end to their visionary dynasty in Mexico. Instead of beholding him upon a throne, they saw him arraigned before the tribunal of justice at Richmond, on a charge of high treason, with Chief Justice Marshall the presiding judge, and John Randolph of Roanoke foreman of the jury. Never, it has been said, did two more wonderful pairs of eyes than those of Marshall and Burr, black, brilliant, and penetrating, look into each other.

In arraigning Burr, there was an element to be reckoned with that is not ordinarily taken into consideration,—the marvellous personality of the man. From his appearance, his manners, his voice, his eyes, emanated an influence not to be lightly estimated. In his bearing and presence he was peerless. He spoke without effort, in a full, crisp, rather than powerful, voice, clothing his thoughts in the language best suited to their most accurate expression, terse, epigrammatic and devoid of figures, his mobile features lending themselves to the thought that was severe or scintillating, tender or impressive. With a woman's tact he combined an adroit intellect equal to any emergency.

He conducted his own defence, supported by the best legal talent in the country. His son-in-law sat beside him every day in court, and Theodosia, the beautiful, noble Theodosia, with sublime faith in her father, inspired a confidence in him in other breasts.

3

She appealed to the poetic fancy of Washington Irving, then a young barrister, who was sent from New York to report the trial for his brother's paper, and whose letters evince an unmistakable sympathy for Burr. Luther Martin, one of the foremost geniuses of the Maryland bar, defended him with an eloquence that rendered Martin himself an object of suspicion to Thomas Jefferson.

" I find that Luther Martin's idolatrous admiration of Mrs. Alston," wrote Blennerhassett, " is almost as excessive as my own, but far more beneficial to his interests and injurious to his judgment, as it is the medium of his blind attachment to her father, whose secrets and views, past, present, and to come, he is and wishes to remain ignorant of. Nor can he see a speck in the character of Alston, for the best of all reasons with him,—namely, that Alston has such a wife."

Though Burr was acquitted, there was an element of hostility to him in the government, and much distrust of him among the people of the country at large. In the following year, therefore, he went to Europe. Theodosia had gone to New York to be near him. He saw her for the last time on June 7, 1808, the night before he sailed. She spent that summer at Saratoga, and the following winter in New York, where she lived in retirement.

" The world," she said, in one of her letters to her father about this time, " begins to cool terribly around me. You would be surprised how many I supposed attached to me have abandoned the sorry losing game of disinterested friendship." She repeatedly urged him to return, promising him that if the worst came to the worst, she would leave everything and suffer with him.

A few months after Madison's elevation to the Presidency she wrote to Mrs. Madison, whom her father had known when she was a young widow, and to whom he had introduced Mr. Madison. "Ever since the choice of the people was first declared in favor of Mr. Madison, my heart, amid the universal joy, has beat with the hope that I, too, should soon have reason to rejoice," she wrote. She desired to know if there was danger of any further prosecution of her father in the event of his return. For the same purpose she wrote two years later from the Oaks, her South Carolina home, to Albert Gallatin, then Secretary of the Treasury, and once a friend of her father's. The letter was calmly logical, yet eloquent with feeling.

In another year Burr was within sight of his home and country. As he neared her shores he wrote in his journal, "A pilot is in sight and within two miles of us. All is bustle and joy except Gamp [the name by which his little grandson called him]. Why should he rejoice?"

Of all the misfortunes of his life, the heaviest were to fall upon him that year. A month after her father's arrival in New York, and while her heart was yet rejoicing that he had been kindly received, the young life of Theodosia's son, full of beauty and promise, closed. "I will not conceal from you," wrote Alston to his father-in-law, "that life is a burden, which, heavy as it is, we shall support, if not with dignity, at least with decency and firmness. Theodosia has endured all that a human being could endure, but her admirable mind will triumph. She supports herself in a manner worthy of your daughter."

Theodosia longed to see her father. We were at war with England at the time, and her husband, governor of his State and general of militia, could not leave his post of duty to accompany her to New York. Her health was so feeble that she could not safely attempt the journey alone. Her father's old friend Timothy Green offered his services, going from New York to bring her north. Under his care, and accompanied by her maid, Theodosia sailed from Charleston on the "Pilot" on the 30th of December, 1812. Save by her fellow passengers on the ill-fated vessel, she was never seen or heard of again. A violent storm swept the coast on the following day, and it has been supposed that the "Pilot," with all on board, went down off Cape Hatteras. After weeks and months of despairing silence, father and husband gave her up. Burr during this period of torturing suspense acquired a habit which clung to him to the end of his life,—of wistfully scanning the horizon for ships as he walked on the battery, then the popular resort of all New Yorkers.

Two or three years after she had gone from their lives, her husband sent a chest of her belongings, which he had not had the courage to open, to her father. "What a fate, poor thing!" sighed Burr, as he recog-

nized the familiar articles. Among the contents was a
letter addressed, " To my husband. To be delivered
after my death and before my burial." It was dated
August 6, 1805, and had been written during an absence of her husband from home, at a time when,
being depressed in health and spirits, she feared that
death was approaching. After leaving some remembrance to the various members of her husband's family,
and begging her husband to provide for Peggy, an old
servant, she says,—

" Death is not welcome. I confess it is ever dreaded.
You have made me too fond of life. Adieu then,
thou kind, thou tender husband. Adieu, friend of my
heart. May Heaven prosper you, and may we meet
hereafter. Adieu; perhaps we may never see each
other again in this world. You are away, I wished to
hold you fast, and prevent you from going this morning. But He who is wisdom itself ordains events; we
must submit to them. Least of all should I murmur,
I, on whom so many blessings have been showered,
whose days have been numbered by bounties, who have
had such a husband, such a child, such a father. Oh,
pardon me, my God, if I regret leaving these. I resign
myself. Adieu once more, and for the last time, my
beloved. Speak of me often to our son. Let him
love the memory of his mother, and let him know how
he was loved by her.

" Your wife, your fond wife,

" THEO.

"Let my father see my son sometimes. Do not be unkind towards him whom I have loved so much, I beseech you. Burn all my papers except my father's letters, which I beg you to return to him. Adieu, my sweet boy. Love your father, be grateful and affectionate to him while he lives, be the pride of his meridian, the support of his departing days. Be all that he wishes, for he made your mother happy."

After expressing a wish that she may not be stripped and washed according to the usual custom, being pure enough to return to dust, she concludes: "If it does not appear contradictory or silly, I beg to be kept as long as possible before I am consigned to the earth."

Alston, who survived her but four years, wrote heartbrokenly to her father: "My boy, my wife, gone both! This, then, is the end of all the hopes we had formed. You may well observe that you feel severed from the human race. She was the last tie that bound us to the species. What have we left? Yet, after all, he is a poor actor who cannot sustain his hour upon the stage, be his part what it may. But the man who has been deemed worthy of the heart of Theodosia Burr, and who has felt what it was to be blessed with such a woman's love, will never forget his elevation."

ELIZABETH PATTERSON

(MADAME JEROME BONAPARTE)

THE city into which Baltimore Town was legislated on the last day of the year 1796 already fostered within its limits the germ of the dual life, social and commercial, to which it has owed its subsequent eminence. Not infrequently, in the days of its inception, the same roof sheltered drawing-room and warehouse, the earlier merchants deeming it necessary to keep their growing interests constantly beneath their personal vigilance. Later, the commercial life crowded out the domestic life, and merchants built their dwellings—stately bricks or frames, painted blue, yellow, or white, facing on avenues of locust-trees—in another part of the town, all bearing quaint evidence of the far-away ports with which their vessels traded, while the whole town was permeated with the odor peculiar to shipping districts.

The first theatre troupe that took the town by storm played in one of the old warehouses, whose walls re-echoed the approbation of the pleasure-hungry audience, among whom were no fastidious critics to pick flaws in " King Richard III.," and still less in " A Miss in her Teens," which followed.

Baltimore never had the qualms of conscience which afflicted some of her puritanical sister towns concerning the pleasures in which she might rightly indulge. She looked out upon life, rather, with a liberality of mental vision which partook of the breadth of the seas her merchantmen traversed.

The brick theatre built in 1781 became one of the most revered spots in the town, and when the actors came her way, Baltimore turned out *en masse* to give them royal welcome.

At the close of the Revolutionary War a number of the French officers of the army and navy who had remained in this country settled in Baltimore, thereby adding a foreign flavor to the social side of its existence, which, like that of all the cities and towns of the young Republic, was characterized more or less by a wholesome simplicity.

In the town, a dozen years before it blossomed into the city, before its streets were paved, when its only communication with inland towns was by means of the stagecoach, and three years before Maryland had ratified the Constitution of the new union of States, there was born to one of her merchants, William Patterson, a daughter, the repute of whose beauty was destined to fill two continents, the spicy aroma of whose wit to penetrate the sacred precincts of imperial throne-rooms, and the story of whose life to touch the hearts of many generations.

The daughter of one of the self-made men whose sterling qualities have lent such stability to the industries and development of the country, who, born of Irish parentage and coming to this country in his fourteenth year, had carved his own way shrewdly and judiciously to the position of distinction he held among his fellow-townsmen and the people of his adopted country, Elizabeth inherited many of his dominant characteristics. He was estimated to be the wealthiest merchant, and, with the possible exception of Charles Carroll, the wealthiest man, in the United States. Her mother, Dorcas Spear, came of good Maryland lineage, and was a woman of gentle character and cultivated mind. She superintended for the most part Elizabeth's education, which, if somewhat erratic, was, nevertheless, superior to that enjoyed by the average woman of that period. It is said that she acquired an early familiarity with Rochefoucauld's " Maxims" and committed to memory Young's " Night Thoughts." Lady Morgan, whose friendship she formed later in life, realizing the brilliancy of her mind, regretted that its earlier direction had not been more systematic.

Her father, from his own statement, seems to have looked after the conduct of his family with the same minute vigilance which he bestowed upon his financial concerns.

" I always consider it a duty to my family," he said, " to keep them as much as possible under my own eye, so that I have seldom in my life left Baltimore either on pleasure or business. Ever since I had a house it has been my invariable rule to be the last up at night, and to see that the fires and light were secured before I retired myself, by which I found little risk from fires and managed to have my family keep regular hours. What I possess is solely the product of my own labor. I inherited nothing of my forefathers, nor have I benefited anything from public favors or appointments."

Strangely similar is the concluding sentiment to that expressed by the founder of another family on another continent,—Napoleon Bonaparte. "Sole fabricator of my destiny, I owe nothing to my brothers," said he, whose fortunes, though he had reared them upon a loftier pinnacle, were, nevertheless, to be crossed by those of the Patterson family.

The eldest daughter in a family of thirteen children, Elizabeth Patterson grew up at a period when the beaux of society read Chesterfield, when no man begrudged the time expended on the profound and sweeping bow then dictated by gallantry, and when fencing and dancing formed a part of every gentleman's education.

"She possessed the pure Grecian contour; her head was exquisitely formed, her forehead fair and shapely, her eyes large and dark, with an expression of tenderness that did not belong to her character ; and the delicate loveliness of her mouth and chin, the soft bloom of her complexion, together with her beautifully rounded shoulders and tapering arms, combined to form one of the loveliest of women." She had had numerous offers of marriage before she reached her eighteenth year, her father's wealth and prominence, independent

Elizabeth Patterson
(Madame Jerome Bonaparte)
From portrait by Quinçon

of her own attractive personality, having insured her social prestige, but as yet she walked heart whole and fancy free.

In the summer of 1803 Jerome, the youngest brother of Napoleon Bonaparte, and then less than nineteen years of age, detaching himself from naval duty in the West Indies and following the bent of his own inclination, eventually put into the port of New York. Whatever breach of military discipline this implies will in no way astound those familiar with Jerome's character.

Too young to have taken part in the struggles that had elevated his family to such dizzy heights, he yet, at an age most susceptible to the altered conditions of his life, came into the full enjoyment of all the advantages they offered. Napoleon was wont to take a humorous rather than a serious view of this " *mauvais sujet*," as he frequently called Jerome. Madame Junot relates a characteristic anecdote in her memoirs which, she says, she had from the Emperor himself. Returning to Paris after the battle of Marengo, Napoleon was presented with various bills contracted by Jerome during his absence. One of these, to the amount of twenty thousand francs, was for a superb shaving set in gold, mother of pearl, silver, ivory, and costly enamels. It was a work of art, but of no possible use to Jerome, who, being but fifteen years old, was without the suggestion of a beard.

To his mother he was an idol, and to the end of her life he was able to extract from her in generous measure much of that substance which she expended grudgingly even upon herself.

Enveloped in the glory of a great name, Jerome's advent into the social current of New York was noised abroad in the few and ordinarily but little-read newspapers of the day.

By stage the news was brought to Baltimore. The returning coach took an urgent invitation to Jerome and his suite to visit that city from Commodore Barney, who had been his recent comrade-in-arms in the West Indies. They accepted the invitation, and early in September found themselves the objects of a lavish hospitality.

Shortly after their arrival one of Jerome's suite, General Rewbell, lost his heart to Miss Henrietta Pascault, one of the belles of the town, to whom he was, after a brief courtship, married.

At the fall races, which were in progress when he arrived in Baltimore, Jerome for the first time saw the woman in whose life he was thereafter destined to play so conspicuous a part. We may well believe that she was radiantly beautiful in a gown of buff silk with a lace fichu and a leghorn hat with tulle trimmings and black plumes.

He had already heard of the beautiful Miss Patterson, and had declared with youthful impetuosity that he would marry her. The fact that she was aware of his preconceived sentiments gave a piquancy to their first meeting, which was enhanced by the boyish enthusiasm with which he referred to her as his "*belle femme.*" The coquetry with which she resisted his too evident admiration had the invariable effect of further ensnaring his princely affections.

They met frequently in those centres of hospitality, the home of Samuel Chase, who twenty-odd years before had put his name to the Declaration of Independence; at " Belvedere," the home of Colonel John Eager Howard, the hero of Cowpens; at " Greenmount," " Druid Hill," and " Brooklandwood," where three other afterwards celebrated beauties were in course of development.

When the festivities in honor of Jerome were at their height, Elizabeth was borne away to the seclusion of a Virginia estate, under the wing of a vigilant mother, who rightly interpreted the course of events and foresaw the obstacles that loomed in the pathway of their happy termination. There only an occasional echo of the gayety that was rife at Baltimore reached her, making unbearable that rural quiet, which means happiness only to a contented mind, and is a veritable torture to such a restless spirit as ever possessed Elizabeth Patterson. Her entreaties at length prevailed, and she was brought back to the city, where, on the 29th of October, to prove how futile the separation had been, scarcely eight weeks after their first meeting, Jerome procured a license of marriage.

He was probably remonstrated with by the members of his suite, whose age and the length of whose friendship made possible that liberty. Rewbell, in the first flush of his own happy union doubtless gave Jerome a reckless support that not even the crafty Le Camus could counterbalance. To such opposition as Elizabeth's family offered, she replied that she " would rather be the wife of Jerome for one hour than of any other man for a lifetime."

On Christmas Eve, 1803, Jerome Bonaparte, brother of the man who five months later declared himself Emperor of France, and Elizabeth Patterson, daughter of an American merchant, entered into that union whose subsequent rending was to echo throughout Christendom. The ceremony was performed in the home of Elizabeth's father, according to the rites of the Catholic Church, by the Right Reverend John Carroll, first archbishop of America. It was witnessed by the French Consul at Baltimore, M. Sotin, Alexander le Camus, who was Jerome's secretary, and the mayor of Baltimore.

The marriage contract, which was drawn up by Alexander J. Dallas, afterwards Secretary of the Treasury, bears evidence of the apprehension felt by Elizabeth's family as to the outcome of this international union with so youthful a bridegroom.

The dress worn by Elizabeth on her bridal night was of exquisitely fine white muslin, elaborately embroidered. She said of the gown in after years that it was one she had frequently worn, as she particularly desired to avoid anything like vulgar display. " And to tell the truth," she added, " there was as little as possible of any gown at all, dress in that day being chiefly an aid in setting off beauty to advantage," which concurs with the statement made by a man who was present at the wedding, to the effect that he could have put all the clothes worn by the bride into his pocket.

The honeymoon days of Jerome and Elizabeth were passed at her father's estate outside of Baltimore, "Homestead." Late in January they were mingling with the merrymakers one afternoon in Market Street. There was good sleighing, and the crisp air rang with the joyousness of an old-time winter. A snowball, sent with the unerring aim and democratic disregard of a small boy of the town, struck Elizabeth. Jerome was outraged at the indignity, and offered a reward of five hundred dollars for the discovery of the youthful miscreant. How trivial seems this "missile light as air" by comparison with those shafts sped later by a not less unerring hand, and striking into the very soul of her womanhood, Jerome making no effort to avert them.

In February this bride and groom of the early century went to Washington, whither since have wended their way so many happy bridal couples. Of the journey there, made in a stage-coach, General Samuel Smith, member of Congress from Maryland, wrote to Mr. William Patterson describing the runaway of the horses as they entered the city and Betsy's presence of mind. The driver having been thrown from his seat, Jerome sprang from the coach with the hope of catching the horses. But as they still sped on, and her danger increased as they penetrated towards the centre of the straggling little capital, Elizabeth opened the door and jumped out into the snow without injury.

While in Washington they were the guests of the French Minister, General Tureau. Aaron Burr, then Vice-President of the United States, meeting Elizabeth at this time, wrote to his daughter Theodosia, whom he thought Elizabeth much resembled, and referred to her as " a charming little woman with sense, spirit, and sprightliness."

Jerome's thoughts were already turning towards France, where every effort was being made to bring about his return—alone. While in New York during the following summer he was made acquainted with the annulment of his marriage, as follows: " By an Act of the 11 Ventose, all the civil officers of the Empire are prohibited from receiving on their registers the transcription of the act of celebration of a pretended marriage that Jerome Bonaparte has contracted in a foreign country during the age of minority, without the consent of his mother and without the publication in the place of his nativity."

In February following the marriage Mr. William Patterson had written to our Minister at Paris, Robert Livingston, enclosing him letters from the President and Secretary of State, to be presented to Napoleon with the hope of obtaining his approval, or at least mitigating any displeasure the marriage might have caused. " I can assure you," he wrote to Livingston, " that I never directly or indirectly countenanced or gave Mr. Bonaparte the smallest encouragement to address my daughter, but, on the contrary, resisted his pretensions by every means in my power consistent with discretion. Finding, however, that the mutual attachment they had formed for each other was such that nothing short of force or violence could prevent their union, I with much reluctance consented to their wishes."

He had, moreover, despatched his eldest son, Robert Patterson, to Paris, to discover which way the wind of the imperial temper blew. As the matter lay rather outside the pale of usual diplomatic issues, it required most delicate manipulation, and while young Patterson received kindly yet cautious expressions of interest and good-will from Napoleon's brothers, an ominous and forbidding silence enveloped the First Consul. His indignation increased with Jerome's continued absence, and when at length he spoke through his Minister of Marine, it was to bid Jerome, as lieutenant of the fleet, to return to France, at the same time forbidding all captains of French vessels to receive on board "the young person to whom Jerome had attached himself." Through the same channel Napoleon offered his forgiveness to Jerome on condition that he abandon Elizabeth and return to France, there to associate himself with his fortunes. Should he persist in bringing her, she would not be allowed to put foot on French territory. Jerome's mother wrote to him at the same time, suggesting that he return to France alone and send his wife to Holland. Robert Patterson, however, who succeeded admirably in keeping himself posted on the variations in the attitude of Jerome's family, advised that Jerome should not return to France without his wife.

Though he made several efforts during the year that

followed to return thither, there is only one on record when it was his purpose to sail alone.

In September, 1804, General Armstrong sailed from New York to replace Livingston at Paris. He had agreed with Jerome to take Madame Bonaparte with him, Jerome himself intending to go on one of the French frigates then in New York harbor. She could thus, at least, have landed in France as a member of the family of the American minister, who might have succeeded in presenting her to Napoleon, with whom she could, no doubt, have pleaded her cause with more effect than could have been produced by any amount of diplomatic correspondence or family intervention. She had the gifts which he most admired in women, great personal beauty and wit, and though the latter might have been too keen for his entire appreciation, she no doubt would have been shrewd enough to temper it to his taste.

She wrote her father from New York, September 5, 1804, of her disappointment at Armstrong's having sailed without her. The reason given was that Jerome and Elizabeth had arrived by stage a few hours after the ship had sailed.

An effort to sail during the following month ended in shipwreck off Pilot Town, where they were finally landed and temporarily housed by one of the inhabitants, on whose clothes-line Madame Bonaparte dried her wardrobe, and from whose hospitable board she enjoyed a dinner of roast goose with apple-sauce, being in exuberant spirits over her rescue.

On March 11, 1805, they finally made their departure from Baltimore in the "Erin," a ship belonging to Mr. Patterson. Though they sailed at an early hour in the morning, and the arrangements for their departure had been conducted with much secrecy, General Tureau wrote from Washington two days later to Mr. Patterson to ask what disposition had been made of Jerome's four carriage-horses, and to suggest, if they were to be sold, that he should like to be considered as a purchaser.

The "Erin" reached Lisbon on April 2, whence Jerome wrote in English to his father-in-law of their safe arrival, and took the opportunity to express his affection for and gratitude towards his second family. He spoke of Elizabeth having been very sea-sick, and added,—

"But you know as well as any body that sea-sick never has killed nobody."

Napoleon's ambassador met the ship upon its arrival, and called upon Elizabeth to ask what he could do for her, addressing her as Miss Patterson.

"Tell your master," she replied, "that Madame Bonaparte is ambitious, and demands her rights as a member of the Imperial family."

She was forbidden to land, and Jerome, taking that farewell of her which fate had destined should be his last, went overland to Paris, while the "Erin" sailed for Amsterdam.

On his way to Paris Jerome met General and Madame Junot *en route* for their new post in Spain. He breakfasted with them and opened his anxious young heart to them, showing them a miniature of Elizabeth, from whom, he declared, nothing should ever separate him.

Upon reaching Paris he went at once to Malmaison and sought an audience with Napoleon, who refused to see him, bidding him write what he wished to say. He wrote, simply announcing his arrival, and received the following reply :

" I have received your letter this morning. There are no faults you have committed which may not be effaced in my eyes by a sincere repentance. Your marriage is null and void, both from a religious and a legal point of view. I will never acknowledge it. Write Miss Patterson to return to the United States, and tell her it is not possible to give things another turn. On condition of her return to America, I will allow her a pension of sixty thousand francs a year, provided she does not take the name of my family, to which she has no right, her marriage having no existence."

From this position Napoleon never swerved. The annuity was paid to Elizabeth after her return to America until the fall of the Empire, and formed the basis of the fortune of one and a half million dollars, accumulated through a long life of frugality and cautious investment, of which she died possessed.

The reply of Pope Pius, to whom Napoleon appealed for the annulment of the marriage, accompanying his request with a costly gold tiara, to the effect that after mature deliberation he had been able to discover no grounds on which the marriage could be cancelled, though it chagrined the Emperor to an extent which he never forgave, did not yet alter the stand he had taken. When Jerome was finally admitted to his presence, he greeted him with that magnetic smile whose potency swayed men and women alike.

"So, sir, you are the first of the family," he said, "who has shamefully abandoned his post. It will require many splendid actions to wipe off that stain from your reputation. As to your love-affair with your little girl, I pay no attention to it."

The "Erin," meanwhile, arrived in the Texel Roads, where, though flying the flag of a friendly power, and a merchant vessel whose clearance from Baltimore showed that she carried no guns, she was placed under guard of two French men-of-war and all communication with the shore prohibited. Through the intercession of Sylvanus Bourne, our Consul at Amsterdam, she was permitted at the expiration of a week to depart, and, bearing her full measure of human desolation, she headed towards the shores of England. The fame of her fair passenger had preceded her, and so large a concourse of people had gathered at Dover to witness the landing of Madame Jerome Bonaparte that Mr. Pitt, then Prime Minister of England, sent a military escort to protect her from possible annoyance of a sympathetic though curious throng.

At Camberwell, near London, her son was born on the 7th of July, 1805, and named Jerome Napoleon.

In June of that year, two months after his return,

Jerome had been restored to his rank in the navy and was cruising off Genoa, whence he wrote, through his secretary, Alexander le Camus, to Mr. William Patterson, of Baltimore, expressing his dissatisfaction at Elizabeth's having gone to England, that country being at the time at war with France. The tone of the letter betrays the change that was already working in Jerome's feelings, though he was at that time sending Elizabeth by every available opportunity messages and pledges of his unswerving love for her.

When we judge him, let us bear in mind not only his youth and all the circumstances of his life, but, above all, that soul-crushing will which he, weakly enough it seems to us, was striving to stand against.

In a subsequent letter to Mr. Patterson, written also by Mr. le Camus, in the course of which Jerome expressed the desire that Elizabeth should return to America and wait there in her own home till he obtained her recall from the Emperor, one feels instinctively that between the lines is written the finale to the short chapter of the romance of Elizabeth Patterson and Jerome Bonaparte.

She returned to her father's home in the fall, though she had written shortly before that she was glad to be among strangers, because " in Baltimore, where people are always on the watch," she would be more observed.

On August 12, 1807, Jerome married Princess Frederika Catherine, daughter of the King of Wurtemberg. As King of Westphalia he offered Elizabeth a home within his dominions, with the title of Princess of Smalcalden and a pension of two hundred thousand francs per year. In regard to the former, she replied that Westphalia was a large kingdom, but not quite large enough for two queens, and with regard to the pension, having already accepted Napoleon's annuity of sixty thousand francs, she made the oft-quoted response that she preferred " being sheltered under the wing of an eagle to being suspended from the bill of a goose."

Napoleon, with his high appreciation of a *bon mot*, desired to know what favor he could bestow upon a woman capable of this witticism. Elizabeth replied through the French Minister at Washington that she was ambitious, and would like to be a duchess.

The Emperor promised the gift, but never conferred it. Notwithstanding her unremitting yet ever futile struggle for recognition, Madame Bonaparte cherished always the most enthusiastic admiration for the genius of the man who had blighted her life. In one of her letters to her father, written from Europe, whither she returned after the fall of the Empire, she said, " They do not in England pretend to revile Napoleon as we have done. His stupendous abilities are admitted; his misfortunes almost respected by his enemies. I listen silently to any discussion in which he bears a part. I easily perceive that he has more justice done him here than with us."

In a subsequent letter she details more fully her attitude towards the entire family.

" I cannot say," she writes, also to her father, " that

I have the least reliance on that family, although I am inclined to reciprocate their kind words and receive their offers of friendship without allowing myself to be deceived by either." And farther on in the same letter she says, in regard to allowing her son to visit Pauline Bonaparte, then the Princess Borghese, at Rome, " My resolution is uninfluenced by personal feelings, never having felt the least resentment towards any individual of that family, who certainly injured me, but not from motives which could offend me. I was sacrificed to political considerations, not to the gratification of bad feelings, and under the pressure of insupportable disappointment became not unjust."

From her letters there seem to have been frequent rumors afloat in regard to her marrying again, both in this country and in Europe, where she was greatly admired. In one letter to her father, written in 1823, she says that while the American newspapers were marrying her she was making her will.

Though she obtained from the Maryland Legislature a divorce, after the fall of Napoleon, it seems to have been rather as a precautionary measure against any possible demands Jerome might make upon her financially than with a view to marrying again.

Tom Moore, whom Lady Morgan sent to her with a letter of introduction, afterwards described her as a beautiful woman, but destitute of all sentiment and with a total disbelief in love, on which, indeed, she bestowed only ridicule. There can be no doubt, however, of the concern and tenderness which she expended upon a dog, Le Loup, which belonged to her son, and which she said was "superior to half the persons one meets in the world." There are many traditions of her wit, which, though tinged with asperity, was ever ready and scintillating. The Honorable Mr. Dundas, who sat beside her at a dinner in London, she speared so unsparingly with the shafts of her sarcasm that his egotism never forgave her. When he asked her, finally, if she had read Captain Basil Hall's book on America, she replied affirmatively. "And did you observe," he continued, bluntly, with the hope of avenging his wounded self-love, "that he called all Americans vulgarians?" "Yes," replied Madame Bonaparte, while the table paused to listen, "and I was not surprised. Were the Americans descendants of the Indians and Esquimaux, I should have been. But being the direct descendants of the English, nothing is more natural than that they should be vulgarians." For both her wit and her beauty she was admired by men and women of fastidious taste, among whom were Sir Charles and Lady Morgan, Talleyrand, Gortschakoff, and Madame de Staël. She so fascinated the Prince of Wurtemberg, uncle of Jerome's second wife, that he confessed his wonderment that Jerome could ever have abandoned her. "Si elle n'est pas reine de Westphalie, elle est au moins reine des cœurs," was Baron Bonsteller's tribute to her.

She seldom alluded to Jerome, though she believed that she always stood first in his heart. She referred in a letter to her father to the probability of his coming to Rome while she was there, but added that she should not see him, "nor would he like it himself after the unhandsome way in which he has always conducted himself. I shall hold my tongue, which is all I can possibly do for him."

Though the greater part of her life was spent in Europe, and she was for a time on terms of considerable intimacy with his family, she met Jerome but once, when they passed each other in the gallery of the Pitti Palace in Florence, Jerome with the Princess Catherine upon his arm. Though they recognized each other, they passed without greeting, Jerome exclaiming, "That was my American wife." Jerome Napoleon, the son of his American wife, was frequently his guest, and was treated with much kindness by the Princess Catherine. Jerome, however, added practically nothing to this son's material comfort, much to his mother's chagrin, and at his death in 1860 it was found that he had not even mentioned his name in his will, a lack of recognition which wounded both mother and son in a more profound sense than his lifelong failure to make provision for him had done. So great was his son's resemblance to his family, and particularly to the Emperor, that the *chargé d'affaires* of France at Amsterdam, in 1820, refused his mother a passport for him to travel through France. It was a strange coincidence that Madame Jerome Bonaparte herself should bear a remarkable resemblance to the Bonaparte family, particularly to Napoleon and Pauline, even having some of their mannerisms.

ELIZABETH PATTERSON

In August, 1855, Louis Napoleon offered to create Jerome Napoleon Bonaparte Duke of Sartène, but he declined the honor, as the object was to take away his name and the rights he possessed as his father's eldest son.

At the request of his half-brother a family council was called, before which the celebrated Berryer pleaded the cause of Madame Jerome Bonaparte and her son, whose rights were ultimately defined as limited exclusively to the use of the name.

On November 3, 1829, Jerome Napoleon Bonaparte, to his mother's intense dissatisfaction and disappointment, married an American, the lovely Miss Susan Mary Williams, of Baltimore. During a long residence abroad Madame Bonaparte had become imbued with the idea that it was a duty her son owed both to her and to himself to ally himself matrimonially with some European family of distinction. Writing to her father from Florence, where she was residing at the time of her son's marriage, she said, " I would rather die than marry any one in Baltimore, but if my son does not feel as I do upon this subject, of course he is quite at liberty to act as he likes best."

Her father died in 1835. He had never been in sympathy with her desire to live in a foreign country, and had frequently upbraided her for her prolonged absence from home. In his will he denounced her as an undutiful daughter, bequeathing her a few small houses besides the home in which she was born, on the east side of South Street, with the lot surrounding it.

In April, 1879, Madame Bonaparte, who was then in her ninety-fifth year, having outlived her son and all of her own generation, passed from the sphere where she had been so conspicuous a figure. She died in a boarding-house in her native city, where she had acquired the reputation of being a keen, eccentric old woman. The sorrows of her youth, belonging to the early days of the country, were too remote to be remembered by her later-day contemporaries, who discovered in her no trace of the bewitching Elizabeth Patterson who had taken by storm the heart of the youthful Prince Jerome.

She rests to-day in Greenmount Cemetery, Baltimore, in a small triangular lot which she selected shortly before her death, saying that as she had been alone in life, so she wished to be in death. On her monument are graven the words that express so much for her,—" After life's fitful fever she sleeps well."

THE CATON SISTERS

AMONG the belles of the early century loom the forms of those gracious women whose names are interwoven with those of the most historic figures of their age, the Caton sisters of Baltimore. Granddaughters of Charles Carroll of Carrollton, one of the most illustrious Americans of the period, they became through marriage identified with the most distinguished families in England.

In 1787 Richard Caton, an Englishman who had settled in Baltimore two years before, and engaged in the manufacture of cotton goods, succeeded in winning the fair hand of Mary Carroll. Rumor said that it had been already partially plighted to her cousin John Car, roll of Duddington Manor. Cousin " Longlegs," however, as Kitty, her irreverent younger sister, called him- was in Europe at the time with her brother Charles, and in those days of slow travel Mary had probably capitulated to the young Briton before John even knew that he had a rival.

Her father, who was reputed the wealthiest man in America, and who provided liberally both for his children and grandchildren, settled upon Mary at the time of her marriage to Richard Caton, the beautiful estate of "Brookland Wood," in the centre of the suburb which has since sprung up and been named for them, Catonsville. Their four daughters were born there and grew up to beautiful womanhood,—Mary, Elizabeth, Louisa, and Emily. They derived every grace of mind and body from a cultivated and accomplished mother who had been educated abroad, and who, accompanying her father to Philadelphia when Congress met there, had known the best there was of social life in America. Closely associated, moreover, from their infancy with their grandfather, a most courtly gentleman, who ever beheld in woman an object worthy of his most chivalrous devotion, they bore every evidence of that innate refinement which created distinction for them in England as the "American Graces."

The life at that time surrounding such men as Carroll was idyllic. Honored by his countrymen, blessed with the wealth giving him every material comfort and luxury, owning his town house, his estate of Doughoregan, and his plantation the famous Carrollton, sought out by the most distinguished men and women at home and from abroad, to say nothing of the myriad resources which such a man as Carroll possessed within himself, he already saw his family—the third generation born in America—well established, with the rooftrees of his son and daughters close by his own. His granddaughters were much with him, and though they were the belles of Baltimore town from their earliest girlhood, a very delightful phase of their life was that portion of it spent on their own and their grandfather's estates. There is frequent mention both in the journal and letters of Charles Carroll of visits from them and also of that princely hospitality that is ever associated with the names of many of the old Maryland estates.

In one letter he alludes to a ball to be given by Captain Charles Ridgley of " Hampton," for which three hundred invitations were out, and to which Mary, Betsy, and Louisa were all going. In another he mentions a ball given by Louisa, who was entertaining the Misses Pinkney at his place at Annapolis.

Many a belle in those days went to balls on horseback with a blanket thrown over her muslin gown to protect it from the dust. Yet it was not too much of an undertaking to go all the way from Annapolis to Baltimore, or *vice versa*, for the pleasure of being present at somebody's ball or dinner-party. Roads and weather permitting, the Catons occasionally made the trip in winter time in a " sled." Roads and weather had much to do with the timing of one's visits in those days of primitive transportation facilities when Charles Carroll recorded that he sent his servant from Donghoregan with a led mare to fetch Miss Nancy Robinson who had been visiting at Homewood, his son's estate.

Nature lent her perfecting hand to the rural life of these people, for nowhere was she ever more munificent in the bestowal of her epicurean gifts than in the State of Maryland, whose lands and whose waters alike cater to the gastronomic proclivities of the *bon vivant*.

Oliver Wendell Holmes at a later period attributed a

lack of appreciation of literature which he fancied he had detected among the Baltimoreans to the preponderance of these very blessings, and suggested that the highest monument in the city should be crowned with a canvas-back duck.

There were club-houses and merrymaking in plenty, with oysters, soft-shell crabs, terrapin, canvas-back ducks, and a roasted young pig with an apple in its mouth, or a turkey stuffed with oysters, as *pièce de résistance*, with a nip of punch for sauce. Miss Ridgley depicts it very temptingly in her little book.

Foremost among the beautiful women whose presence lent piquancy to this life were the Catons. In 1807 Mary, who was at the time nineteen years old, was married to Robert Patterson, the eldest son of William Patterson. She thus became the sister-in-law of the unhappy Madame Jerome Bonaparte, between whom and herself there seems to have existed no great sympathy, through no fault of Mary Caton's.

The event was a welcome one to William Patterson, who was at the time the wealthiest merchant in America. The wedding ceremony was performed in the private chapel of the Carroll family by Archbishop Carroll, who four years previously had similarly united Elizabeth Patterson and Jerome Bonaparte. In April, 1811, Robert and his wife, accompanied by her sisters Elizabeth and Louisa, went abroad, sailing from Baltimore on one of his father's ships and landing in Lisbon in the latter part of May. Robert Patterson had already travelled and lived much in Europe. To the Catons it

Mary Caton
(Lady Wellesley)
From portrait by Sir Thomas Lawrence

was the first of a series of numerous trans-Atlantic trips.

While in Spain they met the Duke of Wellington, who was there at that time conducting the peninsular war, and Colonel Sir Felton Bathurst Hervey, who had been his aide-de-camp at Waterloo and whom Louisa Caton afterwards married. Charles Carroll, writing of Hervey after his marriage to Louisa, which occurred on the 1st of March, 1817, said, "All who know him love him." He was a gallant soldier and had lost his right arm at Vittoria.

The Duke of Wellington's ardent admiration for Mrs. Patterson drew him within the wake of the little American party as they progressed in their travels over Europe, lending them the prestige which opened for them the most exclusive houses in England. Apparent as his admiration was, not the least breath of scandal ever touched the name of this beautiful young matron. The Prince Regent, to whom Wellington presented her, spoke later to Richard Rush, the American Minister, of her unusual beauty. When she came, later in life, into contact with William IV. as first lady in waiting at Windsor, she won the sincere admiration of that sovereign on account of the high standard of morality which she maintained.

After the marriage of Hervey and Louisa Caton they were entertained by the Duke of Wellington at Walmer Castle. The Duchess of Rutland gave them a ball, and bestowed upon the sisters on that memorable night the title under which they became famous,—

the "American Graces." Hervey's death occurred in 1819, and Robert Patterson's at Baltimore in the fall of 1822. The widow of the latter shortly afterwards rejoined her sisters in England, where they were again entertained at Wellington's country-seat. While there they met for the first time his eldest brother, Richard Wellesley, Earl of Mornington, and like himself a soldier and a statesman. In 1797 he had been made Governor of India by George III., who, in return for the services he rendered there, had created him Marquis of Wellesley. At the time he met Mrs. Patterson and her sisters he was Lord Lieutenant of Ireland. Two years later, when Mrs. Patterson and Elizabeth Caton visited Dublin, he entertained them royally, bestowing the most devoted attentions upon the former, to whom he subsequently offered himself.

After a brief engagement they were married at the viceregal castle, the ceremony being performed twice, to accord with the religious convictions of both the bride and the groom, the Archbishop of Dublin marrying them according to the rites of the Catholic Church, and the Lord Primate of Ireland according to those of the Church of England.

Unusual magnificence marked the festivities which followed this event, as well as those of the remainder of Lord Mornington's reign as viceroy.

On July 4, 1827, Bishop England, of South Carolina, gave the following toast to Charles Carroll, who was the last survivor of the signers of the Declaration of Independence: "To Charles Carroll of Carrollton:

in the land from which his grandfather fled in terror his granddaughter now reigns a queen."

It was rather a strange coincidence that two daughters of the little American town of Baltimore, Elizabeth Patterson and Mary Caton, neighbors and contemporaries, should have married brothers of two of the most formidable characters in modern history,—Napoleon Bonaparte, the self-styled conqueror of the world, and the Duke of Wellington, his conqueror.

Madame Jerome Bonaparte, who was in Europe at the time of her sister-in-law's second marriage, thus wrote to her father concerning it:

"HAVRE, November 21, 1825.

"DEAR SIR,—I write by this packet to announce to you the marriage of Mrs. Robert Patterson. Mrs. Brown received a letter from Betsy Caton the day on which it was to take place. She has made the greatest match that any woman ever made. . . . The Marquis of Wellesley is Lord Lieutenant of Ireland. He is sixty-five. He married an Italian singer, by whom he had a family of children. She is dead. He has no fortune. On the contrary, he is over head and ears in debt. His salary is £35,000 per annum as Lord Lieutenant of Ireland. He will be there eighteen months longer, and if the King does not give him another place he is entitled as a poor nobleman to at least a thousand pounds a year. He is brother of the Duke of Wellington. Mary's fortune is reported in Europe to be £800,000 cash. It has been mentioned in all the papers at that sum."

Wellesley retained his position in Ireland till 1828. He was then appointed Controller of the Royal Household of William IV., and his wife first lady in waiting at Windsor Castle. Wellesley's death occurred in 1842, the Marchioness surviving him over eleven years. The latter part of her life was spent at the Royal Palace at Hampton Court, where Queen Victoria presented her with a house in recognition of her husband's services.

Louisa Caton was married for the second time in 1828 to the eldest son of the Duke of Leeds, Francis Godolphin D'Arcy Osborne, Marquis of Carmarthen, who came into his title and estates ten years later.

This marriage called forth another letter from Madame Jerome Bonaparte to her father: "Louisa has made a great match. He is very handsome, not more than thirty-eight, and will be a duke with £30,000 a year."

Elizabeth Caton married once, and that much later in life than her sisters. She became, in 1836, the wife of Baron Stafford, whose family name was Jerningham.

Emily Caton, the youngest of the four sisters, and the only one who left descendants, married John Mac-Tavish, a Scotchman, who had settled in Canada, whence he was sent as consul to Baltimore. Josiah Quincy, who met her at dinner at her grandfather's in 1826, recorded in his journal that he had been much impressed with her air of high breeding.

MARGARET O'NEILL

(MRS. JOHN H. EATON)

TO the student of social history few careers surpass in interest that of Margaret O'Neill. Born of humble parentage, she ran the gamut of social possibilities, exercising more influence over the political destinies of her country than any other American woman has ever done.

Unlike other great belles who owe their fame to the universal admiration they evoke, Margaret O'Neill owed hers quite as much to the animosity she roused. Her cause hotly espoused by the President of the United States, her conduct made the subject of cabinet debates, she rose to fame as broad as the land of her birth, and later beyond the seas to a fame unshadowed by enmity, though not dearer to her patriotic soul. Born late in the last century, she came to be a belle in so far as having beaux makes a girl a belle in the days when the native Washington girl had few rivals. The shriek of Fulton's steamboat had not yet startled the world. The stage-coach was the universal means of conveyance, though the daughters of some Southern and Western Congressmen, from districts unfamiliar even with its lumbering proportions, ambitious to taste the pleasures of a season at the capital, used frequently to make the tedious journey on horseback. Her girlhood belleship had well terminated, indeed she had married and brought children into the world, before the completion of the great canal in 1826, which made the more sanguine voyager of that day hopeful that eventually eight miles might be travelled in an hour !

Though she never knew the exact date of her birth, she had heard it frequently related that she was two weeks old at the time of Washington's funeral, December 18, 1799. She was the eldest daughter of William O'Neill, a descendant of the O'Neills of Ulster County, Ireland, and himself a native of New Jersey, who had migrated to the capital with the hope of improving his fortunes. There he opened a tavern in the western section of the city, a short half-mile from the President's house. He was a genial host, and his house soon attained popularity with the *jeunesse dorée*, as well as with military men and Congressmen, though it was a long way from the Capitol. The Union Tavern, in Georgetown, however, which was also popular with our early law-makers, was still farther away. From its door to the Capitol the old 'bus known as the Royal George, one of Washington's earliest institutions, made frequent trips, stopping at O'Neill's and other taverns and boarding-houses along the route to pick up its patrons.

Margaret grew up in the unconventional atmosphere of the tavern, a type of undisciplined American girlhood, wayward, high spirited, full of generous impulses, her mind fed on impetuous and misguided admiration, and herself blessed with a magnetic soul that drew most men and many women irresistibly to her. She was a toast that stirred the hearts of the most phlegmatic of mankind and evoked unparalleled enthusiasm from those of more ardent temperament. Hers was the highest type of Irish beauty, a marvellously white skin, soft gray eyes, warm chestnut hair that curled above an expressive brow, exquisite features, a small round chin, a delicately beautiful figure of medium height, with an erect carriage and her spirited head nobly poised.

The "Health," written by Edward C. Pinkney, whom Edgar Allen Poe placed first in his estimate of lyric poets of America, is said to have been inspired by her in 1824.

"I fill this cup to one made up of lovliness alone,
  A woman, of her gentle sex the seeming paragon,
  To whom the better elements and kindly stars have given
  A form so fair that, like the air, 'tis less of earth than heaven.

"Her every tone is music's own, like those of morning birds,
  And something more than melody dwells ever in her words ;
  The coinage of her heart are they, and from her lips each flows,
  As one may see the burthened bee forth issue from the rose.

"Of her bright face one glance will trace a picture on the brain,
  And of her voice, in echoing hearts a sound must long remain ;
  And memory such as mine of her so very much endures,
  When death is nigh, my latest sigh will not be life's, but hers.

" Affections are as naught to her, the measure of her hours ;
    Her feelings have the fragrancy, the freshness of young flowers.
    And lovely passions, changing oft, so fill her, she appears
    The image of themselves by turns the idol of past years.

" I filled this cup to one made up of loveliness alone,
    A woman, of her gentle sex the seeming paragon.
    Her health !   And would on earth there stood some more of such
        a frame,
    That life might be all poetry and weariness a name."

She went to school at Mrs. Hayward's seminary, and later to Mr. Kirk.   She also attended a dancing-school that gave exhibitions of the grace and proficiency of its pupils in the parlors of the Union Tavern in Georgetown.   At one of these exhibitions Margaret was crowned by Mrs. Madison, the wife of the President, as the prettiest girl and most graceful dancer in the room.   Naturally ambitious, this first social triumph pointed out the possibility of greater ones, to be achieved only after bitter contests that would have crushed the spirit of a more sensitive woman.

Her father deeming her sufficiently well educated, in which opinion she concurred, she quitted school in her fifteenth year, and, being now a young woman of bewitching beauty and abundant leisure, she entered extensively upon her career as a belle.

Two young military men whom her fascinations had ensnared were at one time on the point of a duel. With one of them, Captain Root, she had planned an elopement, and was actually about to descend from her window when she accidentally overturned a flower-pot: this crashing on the ground below, roused her father and put an end to her flight. More than that, her indignant parent carried her off to New York, where he left her under the wing of his old friend Governor De Witt Clinton, to go to Madame Nau's school. Clinton was very severe with the spoiled little beauty, and the staid atmosphere of his home was not congenial to her. She wrote her father very homesick letters, in one of which she promised that if he would take her home "neither Root nor branch should ever tear her from him." Her wit greatly pleased him, and after he had passed the *bon mot* around among his guests and his Peggy's admirers, he went to New York and brought her home.

It has been said that she was not yet sixteen when from a window of her father's tavern she for the first time saw John Bowie Timberlake, as he passed along Pennsylvania Avenue on horseback. Their acquaintance, engagement, and marriage followed within the space of a few weeks.

Several years of quiet happiness ensued, during which three children, a son, who died in infancy, and two daughters, were born to them.

Timberlake was a purser in the navy, and when he was ordered to sea duty he closed his little home, and his wife and children went to her father's to stay during the time of his absence. He died of asthma aboard the " Constitution," at Port Mahon.

His widow shortly afterwards married General Eaton,

who was at that time a United States Senator and a guest at her father's house. For the first time the little Peggy O'Neill, of triumphant dancing-school days, felt that her foot was actually upon the rounds of the social ladder. John Quincy Adams was President at the time, and one of the bitterest Presidential campaigns this country has ever witnessed had just drawn to a close in the election of Jackson. One victim of the freedom of press and speech, everywhere indulged in, was the wife of the President-elect. Her gentle soul, stung by the breath of slander, which all the vigilance of a devoted husband had been powerless to avert, had passed unregretfully from earth. Jackson came to Washington a bereaved and embittered man.

There was a puritanical tendency among the women who made up the society of that era, and to whom Margaret O'Neill appeared as the embodiment of a sport-loving element that prevailed among men.

Life had a rural quality in those days which it has since lost. Horse-racing was universal, and the great race between Eclipse and Sir Henry, run on Long Island May 27, 1823, for a purse of ten thousand dollars, was a national event. Hundreds of thousands of dollars had been staked, and Peggy O'Neill no doubt was intimately acquainted with some of the heaviest winners and losers, among the latter of whom was John Randolph. Though she was far too young to remember the opening of the first race-track in Washington, November 3, 1803, she was yet familiar with all the details of its inauguration, on which occasion both houses of

Congress had adjourned, the Senate to have the ceiling repapered, and the House, which was apparently less resourceful, because it had no pressing business on hand.

Growing up in a public house, she was undoubtedly familiar with much in the lives of men of which other women of her day, leading more secluded lives, feigned ignorance. Yet she had become in no way contaminated by the liberal atmosphere she had breathed from infancy.

General Eaton and his bride returned from their honeymoon shortly before Jackson's inauguration. A few of the Senators' wives called upon her, but she was generally not well received, and slander had already begun its mischievous work when Jackson appeared in Washington and swore " by the Eternal" that his little friend, whom he had known all her life, should not be defamed.

Her name was already on every lip at the capital, and there is no doubt that as many went to Jackson's inauguration ball to see her as to see the President. They stood on chairs and benches in their efforts to catch a glimpse of her, and she made a picture worthy of their endeavors, in her pink gown, with her headdress of nodding black plumes.

Eaton was made Secretary of War. He was Jackson's old friend, and had labored unremittingly for his election. Moreover, thought the chivalrous old President, this would insure Mrs. Eaton's triumph. The women of the cabinet, however, refused to recognize her. Though Mrs. Calhoun, the wife of the Vice-

President, had called upon her as a Senator's wife, she declined to associate with her as the wife of a cabinet minister. Calhoun, to whom an appeal was made, declared himself powerless, as " the quarrels of women, like those of the Medes and Persians, admitted of neither inquiry nor explanation."

Van Buren, Secretary of State, and Barry, Post-Master-General, the former a widower and the latter a bachelor, stood aloof from the tempest in which their fellow-officials were engulfed. That astute politician and prince of diplomats, Martin Van Buren, won Jackson's undying friendship by the warmth with which he took up his friend's cause. He had been a beau at evening functions when he was in the Senate, and he knew the social status of every one at Washington, and precisely what brought every stranger to the capital. While he admired Mrs. Eaton and desired to defend her, he also undoubtedly realized all the advantages to be gained by such a course.

The spirit of hostility gradually spread to every branch of society. The Diplomatic Corps became involved; Vaughn, the British minister, and Baron Krudner, the Russian envoy, both bachelors, ranged themselves beneath Mrs. Eaton's standard. They féted and dined her, and gave her substantial evidence of their adherence to her cause. Huygens, the Dutch minister, having a wife who belonged to the opposition, was less fortunate. Finding herself placed next to Mrs. Eaton at dinner on one occasion, Mrs. Huygens took her husband's arm and turned her back upon the assemblage. While all who witnessed the affront were appalled into an awkward silence, Mrs. Eaton, following the retreating form with critical eyes, commented admiringly upon her fine carriage.

Between her defenders and her defamers her Celtic blood bore her up, and her sunny soul lost none of its serenity. One of Jackson's biographers, however, states that when the matter reached the ears of the irate President, he threatened to demand Huygens's recall unless he and his wife forthwith apologize to Mrs. Eaton.

The contest waxed warmer day by day, both houses of Congress furnishing recruits to one side or the other.

The cabinet was dubbed the "Petticoat Cabinet," and Mrs. Eaton's fame as Bellona, the Goddess of War, spread through the land. Calhoun attacked the President for retaining in his cabinet an element of so much discord. But Jackson was a true knight, and his friendship was stanch.

The bitter feeling, meanwhile, among the cabinet ministers had attained such a pitch that they could no longer come together amicably. Their resignations were tendered to the President and accepted, and a new cabinet was formed.

It was during a recess of Congress. Van Buren was sent as minister to England, where he was cordially received. When Congress reassembled, however, the Senate refused to confirm his appointment, Calhoun casting the decisive vote.

A letter of Daniel Webster's, written about this time, reveals the seriousness of the situation. "It is odd enough," he wrote, "that the consequences of this dispute in the social and fashionable world are producing great political effects, and may very probably determine who shall be successor to the present Chief Magistrate." And they did. Jackson's power and popularity were such that he was in a position to dictate to his party the choice of his successor. His choice fell upon Van Buren, who had undoubtedly labored for him in the days of his bitter fight for the Presidency, and who had further and effectually endeared himself to his chief by his zealous defence of Mrs. Eaton, who in Jackson's eyes was not only a fair and beautiful woman, but the representative of oppressed womanhood.

General Eaton was appointed governor to the Territory of Florida, and later he was sent as our minister to the court of Madrid.

This ended Mrs. Eaton's social conflict. She was graciously received and universally admired in that land of aristocrats, and her long residence there and in Paris, whither she went before returning to this country, formed one of the happiest periods of her life.

One of her daughters, the beautiful Virginia Timberlake, familiarly known among the men and women who were young with her, as "Ginger" Timberlake, married the Duke de Sampoyo and went to live in France, where, in turn, one of her daughters has recently married a son of the elder Rothschild. Margaret, Mrs. Eaton's second daughter, married one of the Virginia Randolphs. To the children by this marriage, deprived by death of both parents, Mrs. Eaton devoted many years of her life. General Eaton died in 1859.

A third marriage contracted by his widow late in life, and subsequently annulled, was productive of much unhappiness in her home.

On the 8th of November, 1879, she reluctantly gave up her hold on life, whose volume had held for her so few blank pages.

In the presence of that foe which every woman fears most, slander, she had never retreated from the position she early determined to carry, and which circumstances proved she was well able to fill. She bore all with a sweet courage, feeling keenly, but not morbidly, the world's sting.

Preserving to the end her wonderful elasticity of spirit, she went out from a life that had been one of alternate turmoil and triumph, beholding only its beauties and loving it to the last. " I am not afraid to die," she said, " but it is such a beautiful world to leave."

CORA LIVINGSTON

(MRS. THOMAS PENNANT BARTON)

CORA LIVINGSTON was born in New Orleans, "the little Paris of America," on the 16th of June, 1806, the year of the great eclipse. Her father, writing to announce her advent to his sister in New York, said God had given him so fair a daughter that the sun had hidden its face.

Though she was a great belle with a national reputation during the decade from 1820 to 1830, those who attempted an analysis of her charm declared that she lacked that attribute which many would esteem the first requisite to belleship,—beauty. Yet she was a notable example of that subtle power that raises a woman above her contemporaries, that evokes an involuntary homage from every eye.

Her mother, writing of her when she was about sixteen and already the belle of New Orleans, to one who had never seen her, said, "She is not a beauty, not a genius, but a good and affectionate child."

Josiah Quincy, that ubiquitous beau who paid his court to the belles of so many cities, seeing her in Washington in 1826, declared that she was not handsome, while he admitted that she was undoubtedly the greatest belle in the United States. " She has a fine figure, a pretty face, dances well, and dresses to admiration," he continued, endeavoring to solve the mystery of the attraction exercised by this exquisite specimen of womanhood. He further confessed that when he left her he bore away an image of loveliness and grace never to be erased, and he went on to quote Burke's apostrophe to the Queen of France,—" Surely never lighted on this orb, which she hardly seemed to touch, a more delightful vision."

She was the daughter of Edward Livingston, a brother of that Chancellor Livingston who, on the 30th of April, 1789, administered the oath of office to the first President of the United States, and of an eminently beautiful creole, Louise Moreau.

Fleeing the terrors of the negro insurrection in San Domingo, Madam Moreau, a young widow, arrived in New Orleans just as the Louisiana purchase was consummated and the province became the property of the United States. French then to the very core, the city has retained evidences of its origin longer than any city of the Union. The thrill of anguish with which it realized that Louisiana had been sold by Napoleon to the United States " on this 9th of July, 1803, at seven P.M.," left its indelible impression upon a people loyal to their nationality and tenacious of its prerogatives.

The wave of emigration which swept into the newly acquired territory from the north bore thither Edward Livingston, of New York. Fortune's reverses had driven him into the new country with the hope of finding there a more promising field for his talent and labors.

The Americans were not well received. Scarcely more than a hundred out of the eight thousand inhabitants had greeted the stars and stripes as they were raised for the first time over the city. So strong, indeed, was the prejudice against them that every unfortunate occurrence was instantly attributed to them. Miss Hunt relates that upon one occasion when a ball was interrupted by an earthquake an indignant old creole gentleman exclaimed that the pleasure of ladies had never thus been interrupted in the days of Spanish or French dominion.

Livingston's knowledge of the language, his tact, his adaptiveness, together with his splendid ability, soon raised him to a conspicuous place at the bar. He was a widower, thirty-nine years of age, when he married Madam Moreau, who was but nineteen. Cora was the only child of this marriage, and ever, even after her own marriage, the inseparable companion of both parents. From her father she derived a sound knowledge of the political questions of the day that made her an intelligent spectator of the historic period in which she lived. From her mother she inherited that grace, mental and physical, that so indelibly impressed her upon the life of which she formed so brilliant a part that her name can no more be eliminated from it than can the names of Andrew Jackson, Martin Van Buren, Daniel Webster, or Henry Clay.

CORA LIVINGSTON

The cultivation of her mind was intrusted to her uncle, Major August Davezac, from whom she received an education of unusual scope. She matured early, being probably more or less at all times a part of the social life that surrounded her parents and into which she made her formal *entrée* at the age of fourteen.

The social atmosphere of New Orleans at this time was like that of no other city on the North American Continent. Creole tastes and institutions were predominant. The only society of the city was Creole, and very delightful and very exclusive it was. The French opera was then, as it has been since, one of its conspicuous features. Tuesdays and Saturdays were the nights when the fashionable world was to be seen in the boxes, and the stage presented nothing more attractive than the beautifully dressed women of the audience, with their artistic coiffures. There were receptions in the boxes between the acts, and a belle's powers of attraction were thus publicly manifested to a people ever ready to add the tribute of its homage.

Cora Livingston before she was sixteen years old, gentle and retiring, shrinking from publicity such as attaches to belles at this end of the century, was known throughout the city of her birth as its greatest belle. In the evenings of the warm season, when the balcony of her house in Chartres Street was converted into a reception-room, in the midst of a devoted family she received not only the admiration of distinguished guests, but the chivalrous and silent homage of many an unknown passer-by.

Frenchmen visiting New Orleans frequently brought letters of introduction from Lafayette to Livingston, whom he had known in New York. Cora thus early became accustomed to an association not only with people of her own city, but with many eminent cosmopolites.

In 1812, when war was declared against England, New Orleans fell into line and gave glorious proof of her loyalty. Her prejudices were swallowed up in the common cause that drew all sections of the country together, and she became in deed, as she already was in name, an American city.

General Jackson's friendship for the Livingstons, of which he gave so many handsome proofs, began at this time.

In 1822 Edward Livingston was elected to Congress, and for eleven years thereafter Washington became his home. While he achieved prominence as a legislator and statesman, the brilliancy of his daughter was acquiring for her a national reputation. He leased the Decatur residence on Lafayette Square, within a stone's throw of the White House, and there gathered about this distinguished family the most cultured element of the Washington of that period,—the Calhouns and their gifted daughter with her perspicuous political theories, the Adamses, Webster, Clay, Chief Justice Marshall, Martin Van Buren, Mrs. Madison, their neighbor across the Park, and the widow of Admiral Decatur.

It was the exception in those days for members of

Cora Livingston
(Mrs. Thomas Pennant Barton)
From miniature by herself

Congress to have their own homes. They lived for the most part in hotels and boarding-houses, and the resident branch of society was more distinctive. Mrs. Decatur, widowed by the famous Bladensburg duel of March 20, 1820, had retired to her estate at Kalorama, which became one of the most delightful centres of resident society. She favored the Livingstons with her sincere regard, and included them among her guests, frequently as often as three times in one week. To stand forth as she does from among the bevy of brilliant women who led the social life of Washington, at a time when conversation was a fine art, deriving a stimulus from such men as Randolph, Pinckney, Webster, and Story, and when women were quite the equals, in wit, humor, and happy rejoinder, of these veteran conversationalists, is an indisputable proof of the superior mental endowments of Cora Livingston.

The Capitol was then as much a feature to the people of Washington as it is to-day to the people outside of Washington. Thither the belles and beaux of the city betook themselves as regularly as the session opened, walking down Pennsylvania Avenue beneath the double row of Lombardy poplars, planted when Jefferson was President. The halls of Congress were smaller and better adapted to both seeing and hearing than they are at present. The discussion of public questions differed also from what one hears nowadays, there being more spontaneity in the oratory and a larger number participating, unless, indeed, there was a grand occasion when the big guns were brought into action, and Clay's mellifluous voice was heard, or Webster's organ notes pealed forth, or Randolph's shrill pipe rent the air.

A distinctive social feature of the time were the assembly balls, held usually at some such place as Carucci's, where Cora Livingston's graceful dancing again made her the cynosure of all eyes. The set in which she danced—there were no round dances in those days—was continually surrounded by admiring spectators, many dancers foregoing that pleasure for the greater one of watching her. Cora Livingston in a ball-gown, going through the stately evolutions of a quadrille, the very embodiment of winsome grace, was a vision that tarried long afterwards with many who so beheld her.

It was at Carucci's in the winter of 1826, when Miss Livingston's belleship was at its height, that the waltz was first seen in Washington. Baron Stoekelburg, of the Russian legation, was its sponsor, and all Washington looked on with dismay, the Baron and his fair partner, whose name has been lost in oblivion, though her temerity should have earned her a better fate, having the floor to themselves.

In 1829 Livingston went into the Senate, and in May, 1831, he succeeded Van Buren as Secretary of State, Van Buren having taken the high ground, so Livingston expressed it, that as a candidate for the Presidency he should not remain in the Cabinet.

In 1833 President Jackson offered Livingston the mission to France. Our affairs with that country were in a complicated condition, and Livingston's patriotism induced him to accept the office.

In April of that year his daughter was married to Thomas Pennant Barton, a son of Dr. Benjamin Barton, of Philadelphia. President Jackson appointed him Secretary of the legation at Paris, sending his appointment enclosed in a note to Cora, that she might have the pleasure of presenting it to him with her own hands. Her intimate acquaintance with the President dated back to her early childhood, when she was scarcely taller than the cavalry boots worn by the hero of the battle of New Orleans, who readily promised to hang Mitchell, the highest English officer among the prisoners, if the British so much as touched a hair of her father's head. He evinced a paternal pride in the adulation she everywhere received as a woman. At his request she stood as godmother to his wife's great niece, Mary Donalson, now Mrs. Wilcox, who was born in the White House during his term of office.

On their return to America, in 1835, both the Livingstons and Bartons made their home at Montgomery Place at Barrytown on the Hudson, an estate of three hundred acres, which Mr. Livingston had inherited from his sister, Mrs. Montgomery, the widow of General Montgomery, of Revolutionary fame.

Mr. Barton was a man of scholarly tastes, to which the tranquil atmosphere of Montgomery Place, with all its historic associations, together with the close companionship of his gifted wife, was an inspiration. He accumulated there a library which, at the time of his death, was considered one of the most valuable private collections in America. He bequeathed it to his wife with the request that she make such disposition of it as best pleased her. Shortly before her death she arranged for its transfer to the Boston Library, where it is preserved, as she knew her husband desired his life work should be, in its entirety, and known as the Barton collection.

In 1870 she went to France to superintend there the publication of a new edition of her father's work on Penal Laws, which appeared simultaneously with an English edition. In France a number of her father's friends were still living, among them Mr. Charles Lucas, of the French Institute, who wrote the Preface to the edition brought out in that country.

Having survived her parents and husband, Mrs. Barton died suddenly at Montgomery Place on the 23d of May, 1873.

The last two winters of her life were spent in Washington, where, at a time when American society was singularly rapid, she shone as the last ray from the glory of an age that was gone, in her whole manner and bearing the unmistakable gentlewoman.

Going one day to her former home, the Decatur House, she requested, without giving her name, that she might be permitted to see the drawing-room. General Beale, who then occupied the house, of which his widow still retains possession, in courteous compliance with her request, led the way thither. As she entered the familiar apartment, memory, conjuring up the forms that were no more, shut out the actual presence of her host. At length regaining her self-possession, she said, " A strange desire has of late possessed me to see again this house in which I spent such happy days. Just where I am standing now I stood thirty-nine years ago and was married." " You then were Miss Cora Livingston," said the general, entering into her mood and reverting instinctively to the days when her scintillating wit had made the name famous, though in the sorrow-laden woman there was no trace of the glorious girl.

EMILY MARSHALL

(MRS. WILLIAM FOSTER OTIS)

BOSTON claims as her own the greatest American man of the nineteenth century, and even with more justice, the most beautiful woman born in America within the same period. "Emily Marshall as completely filled the ideal of the lovely and feminine, as did Webster the ideal of the intellectual and the masculine," Quincy, a native of the same State, has written of her, adding that though superlatives were intended only for the use of the very young, not even the cooling influences of half a century enabled him to avoid them in speaking of her.

He never forgot the first time he saw her walking on Dover Street Bridge, Boston's fashionable promenade in those days. "Centuries are likely to come and go," he continued, "before society will again gaze spellbound upon a woman so richly endowed with beauty as was Miss Emily Marshall. She stood before us, a reversion to that faultless type of structure which artists have imagined in the past, and to that ideal loveliness of feminine disposition which poets have placed in the mythical golden age."

Daniel Webster upon one occasion, during his residence in Boston, entered the old Federal Street Theatre, and was hailed with cheers. A few minutes later Emily Marshall appeared in her box, when the entire audience rose as one man and offered her the same homage it had bestowed upon Webster. To us who look back upon her, through nearly three-quarters of a century, she stands forth in such exquisite relief from her environment that we are conscious of it only where the light of her beguiling presence touches it.

She was the daughter of Josiah Marshall, a Boston merchant in the China trade, a man of sagacity and enterprise in business affairs, and possessed of those traits that made him a most lovable father, wisdom, benevolence, and gentleness, with a quaint humor and readiness in *repartée* that enhanced the bond of comradeship between himself and his children.

The people of his own State, as well as the inhabitants of the far-away Sandwich Islands, are indebted to him for many benefactions. To the latter his ships carried the first missionaries, the materials for the first houses erected there, and the carpenters to build them. Upon being charged duty on some salmon which he had imported from the Columbia River, he pointed out to Louis Cass the desirability of establishing the claim of the United States to the region of Oregon.

In the improvements which added so much to the prosperity of Boston in 1826 he was Mayor Quincy's constant adviser and abettor.

He was a handsome man, with firm mouth and kindling eyes, and his quick step was well known in the business world, where to many a young man he gave the opportunity which was the opening of a successful mercantile career.

He was a son of Lieutenant Isaac Marshall of the Revolutionary army, and a great-grandson of John Marshall, one of the founders of Billerica, Massachusetts, in which town he was born. In the year 1800 he married Priscilla Waterman, a daughter of Freeman Waterman, who represented the town of Halifax in the Cambridge Convention which ratified for Massachusetts the Constitution of the United States.

Waterman had a sister who was distinguished for her charm, and who married a Mr. Josselyn. Traditions of the Josselyn beauty lingered in Plymouth until Emily Marshall's time. Mrs. Marshall was a woman of much beauty, grace, and dignity.

Emily was born in the year 1807 on an estate at Cambridge, which had been laid out a century before by Thomas Brattle. Shortly after her birth her parents moved into a house in Brattle Square, Boston, known as the White House. It was built upon a terrace, with steps running down to the square. A large, old-fashioned garden in the rear was one of its attractions. The house had already had two distinguished tenants, Lieutenant-Governor Bolin and John Adams, the latter having lived there when he was a young lawyer.

When Emily was fourteen years old her family once more transplanted their household gods, going this time into the house on Franklin Place, to which her beauty brought such fame. It had already begun to manifest itself, and when she was but nine or ten years of age she was frequently stopped on the street by strangers, who asked whose child she was and involuntarily told her of her budding loveliness. Yet so unconscious did she ever appear of its possession, so wholly lacking in personal vanity, that one of her sisters, gazing upon her one night arrayed in a ball gown, and unable to restrain her admiration, asked her if she realized how beautiful she was. "Yes," she replied, "I know that I am beautiful, but I do not understand why people act so unwisely about it."

Her education was begun at Madame English's school, where Russell Sturgis, afterwards a partner of the Barings, said he first made her acquaintance. Like every one else who ever saw her, he never forgot her. More than forty years after her death, writing to thank her daughter for the photograph of a portrait she had sent him, he said, "I remember perfectly the portrait and the time when it was painted. No painter could ever give the brilliant expression which always lighted her beautiful face ; the portrait is as good, therefore, as any one could make it."

At Dr. Park's school on Mount Vernon Street, then one of the best girls' schools in Boston, Margaret Fuller was one of her school-mates, and confessed later to a sister of Emily's that she would willingly have changed her mental gifts for those of the beauty and magnetism with which Emily was endowed.

From Dr. Park's Emily went to Madame Canda's French school on Chestnut Street. Her musical education, which continued till the time of her marriage, was conducted by Mr. Matthew, Mademoiselle Berthien, and Mr. Ostinelli.

The long acquaintance existing for generations among the families and individuals who made up the Boston society of Emily Marshall's day, had instilled into it a spirit of delightful simplicity. A traveller from Great Britain who visited the United States early in the century declared that all the people of the Bay State called one another by their Christian names.

Dinner-parties were daylight affairs, beginning usually not later than four o'clock. The dinner was served in courses, beginning with soup, which was followed frequently by a corn-meal pudding designed for the avowed purpose of mitigating the appetite before the introduction of the roast, which was carved upon the table by the host, and served with Madeira, port, or sherry.

One of Harrison Gray Otis's favorite after-dinner stories, which he told in his own matchless way, was of the first appearance of champagne in Boston. It was introduced by the French consul, the unsophisticated Bostonians partaking of the palatable beverage with all the confidence which they were wont to bestow upon cider, of which they thought it to be only a mild form and of foreign extraction.

From eight until twelve were the hours for balls, at which girls out for the first time wore white book-muslin frocks, the belles of a season or more appearing in tarleton, and dancing out a pair of slippers in an evening, slippers then being made with paper soles and no heels. Light refreshments, such as nuts, raisins, or oysters, were served at these evening affairs, and were passed on trays, there being no elaborately set supper-tables.

The five-o'clock tea, now so prevalent throughout the country, made its way first into Boston and New York, where it appeared in all its native English simplicity.

From England also came actors bringing us our first conception of Shakespearean characters, Cooper interpreting Hamlet to a Boston audience in 1807, the year Emily Marshall was born, followed by Wallack, Edmund Kean, Charles Matthews, the comedian, and Phillips, with his infectious songs, the echoes of such refrains as "Though love is warm awhile" floating long after from drawing-room, nursery, and kitchen.

From the mother-country came our literature of the early century, Scott, the new writer, being much read, also Fanny Burney, Jane Austen, Maria Edgeworth, and Shakespeare always.

Boston early achieved her reputation as a patroness of letters. At her noted seat of learning not only the youth of America, but a number of foreigners were even then educated. Many an American boy who claimed Harvard as his Alma Mater had journeyed to her sacred precincts, when the country was in its teens, all the way from the wilds of Kentucky on horseback.

Commencement day was a State holiday, when the flower of Massachusetts womanhood united to do honor to the occasion. Many a man went thence on his way with a face enshrined in his memory that he had not found in his Virgil or his Homer, though nothing more perfect graced those classic pages than the face of Emily Marshall.

Though Willis's sonnet speaks of her eyes as hazel, they have been described elsewhere as black. It is probable that their color varied and intensified with every thought or emotion. Her hair was of that golden brown that flashes like bronze in the sunlight. In height she was five feet and five inches. "Her personal grace," said one of her admirers, a judge of the Supreme Court of Pennsylvania, "was not acquired; a creature of such absolute natural perfection was physically unable to make an ungraceful movement."

One who knew her in daily life writes: "The unspeakable grace, the light of the eye, the expression of the face, they come back to me as I think of her, but I cannot convey them to others. It was the light in a porcelain vase. You could draw the outlines of the vase, but when the light was quenched it could be known no more."

Enshrined in this form of almost unearthly loveliness was a spirit of even rarer beauty, a character that would have made even an ugly woman a force. In every relationship she wielded an exquisite influence. With a nature profoundly and silently religious were combined a high sense of duty, a ready sympathy, an absolute frankness and simplicity, a clear, practical judgment, and a rapid insight into character.

In conversation she drew out the best thoughts of others intuitively and without vanity, reserving her own brilliant intellect and ready wit for those who really enjoyed it.

To her children, her self-abnegation, her gentleness, her faultless judgment, the intense womanliness of her nature, made her an ideal mother. She was as tenderly loved by women as she was chivalrously worshipped by man. Her twenty-nine years of life were all too short for those who prized and lost her.

"Say that no envious thought could have been possible in her presence," is another woman's tribute to her; "that her sunny ways were fascinating to all alike; that she was as kind and attentive to the stupid and tedious as if they were talented and of social prominence." Of the effect everywhere produced by so exquisite a personality there are countless evidences. It was not restricted to any age, sex, or social class. Mr. William Amory claims to have been in his youth the most distinguished man in Boston, because he was not in love with Emily Marshall.

A carpenter, whose shop was near the house in which she lived after her marriage, failed to go home to his dinner one day, and being asked the reason, replied that he had seen Mrs. Otis go out earlier in the day and he hoped that she might come back that way, adding that he would rather see her any day than eat his dinner.

Franklin Place became the favorite walk with the young men of Boston, many of whom never failed once or twice daily to pass her house, with the hope of catching a glimpse of her at one of its windows. Dr. Malcolm's church, of which she was a member, also added many devotees to its congregation, William Lloyd Garrison being among the number, who confessed that he occasionally went there with the hope of seeing the lovely face of Emily Marshall.

Nor was the repute of her beauty confined to her native city. Wherever she went her unusual presence was instantly felt ; she needed no society correspondent to herald her, no princely admirer to create prestige for her. Her claim to the world's homage was self-evident. She was a queen in her own right.

When she visited Philadelphia, so great was the desire to see her that the young girls were let out of school before the usual closing hour, that they might have an opportunity to see her as she passed along the street.

While she was at Saratoga, " gay, amusing, and confusing," reached in those days from Boston by a tedious stage-coach ride across the country, she never left the hotel nor returned to it without attracting a throng of people, eager even for a passing glimpse of her.

Nathaniel Parker Willis, who once had made a journey in the same coach in which Emily Marshall and her mother were travelling, related afterwards that wherever the coach stopped for dinner the news of the marvellous beauty of one of the passengers was spread abroad so rapidly that by the time Miss Marshall returned to her seat in the coach a great crowd of people would be assembled to see her.

EMILY MARSHALL

The following is Willis's very pretty acrostic on Emily Marshall, which is included in his published verses in the form of a sonnet:

> " Elegance floats about thee like a dress,
>   Melting the airy motion of thy form
> Into one swaying grace, and loveliness,
>   Like a rich tint that makes a picture warm,
> Is lurking in the chestnut of thy tress,
>   Enriching it as moonlight after storm
> Mingles dark shadows into gentleness.
>   A beauty that bewilders like a spell
> Reigns in thine eyes' dear hazel, and thy brow,
>   So pure in veined transparency, doth tell
> How spiritually beautiful art thou,—
>   A temple where angelic love might dwell,
> Life in thy presence were a thing to keep,
> Like a gay dreamer clinging to his sleep."

Percival's sonnet, published in the *Literary Gazette* of Philadelphia, August, 1825, is perhaps the best known of the poetical outpourings which her loveliness inspired. It also is an acrostic.

> " Earth holds no fairer, lovelier than thou,
>   Maid of the laughing lip and frolic eye ;
> Innocence sits upon thy open brow
>   Like a pure spirit in its native sky.
> If ever beauty stole the heart away,
>   Enchantress, it would fly to meet thy smile;
> Moments would seem by thee a summer's day
>   And all around thee an Elysian isle.

Roses are nothing to thy maiden blush
   Sent o'er thy cheek's soft ivory ; and night
   Has naught so dazzling in its world of light
As the dark rays that from thy lashes gush.
   Love lurks among thy silken curls and lies,
   Like a keen archer, in thy kindling eyes.''

William Foster Otis, to whom she was married in May, 1831, first saw her when she was fourteen years old, on her way home from school. He loved her from the moment his eyes fell upon her, and honored her with the loyalty of a lifetime, though death robbed him of her five years after their marriage.

Of the wedding there is extant a very good description in the form of a letter written by the bridegroom's sister, under date of May 20, 1831.

"There were fifty guests at the wedding, an enormous crowd at the visit [reception] which kept us until half-past ten from supper. The bride looked very lovely, and was modest and unaffected. Her dress was a white crêpe lisse, with a rich vine of silver embroidery at the top of the deep hem. The neck and sleeves were trimmed with three rows of elegant blond lace very wide. Gloves embroidered with silver, stockings ditto. Her dark-brown hair dressed plain in front, high bows with a few orange-blossoms and a rich blond lace scarf, tastefully arranged on her head, one end hanging front over her left shoulder, the other hanging behind over her right. No ornaments of any kind, either on her neck or ears, not even a buckle. I never saw her look so beautiful. Every one was remarking on her beauty as they passed in and out of the room. Mrs. Marshall [the bride's mother] looked extremely handsome. William [the bridegroom] looked quite as handsome as the bride, and seemed highly delighted. The bride and groom went to their house alone [70

Beacon Street] about one o'clock [in the morning]. The groomsmen serenaded them until the birds sang as loud as their instruments."

James Freeman Clarke, who was present at her wedding, said afterwards that he " had often been perplexed at the accounts he had read of the great personal power of Mary Queen of Scots. He had never been able to comprehend how the mere beauty of a woman could so control the destinies of individuals and nations, causing men gladly to accept death as the price of a glance of the eyes or a touch of the hand." After he had beheld Emily Marshall, however, he realized the possibilities of such a power that is not created once in a century.

She died in 1826, leaving two daughters and an infant son.

> " She had no autumn, not a storm
>   Darkened her youthful happiness ;
> No winter came to bend that form,
>   Or silver o'er a silken tress.

> " We miss her when we gaze on beauty's throng,
>   We miss her, aye, and we shall mourn her long.
> Yet mourn her not, she had the best of life ;
> A tender mother and a happy wife."

The above lines were written by her friend Fanny Inglis, afterwards Madame Calderon de la Barca.

The chivalrous devotion which her daughters call forth, after more than threescore years, from the men who knew her is in itself sufficient to place her among the classics of American womanhood.

OCTAVIA WALTON

(MADAME LE VERT)

INTO a world in which so many are born strangers, some later to know it in part and others destined to remain forever out of touch with life, and lonely spectators rather than a part of it, Octavia Walton came as unto her own. Every atom of her being was in absolute accord with the universe. No bristling antipathies hedged in her genial personality nor raised barriers between herself and the beauties of life. She perceived them always and with an enthusiasm that raised not only her own existence, but that of many others, above the level of the commonplace. She was a sort of social sun, radiating light, warmth, and beauty upon all the lives that touched hers, and it has been said that no one ever came in contact with her, of no matter what rank or condition in life, without experiencing a sense of elation. She was one of nature's cosmopolites, a woman to whom the whole world was home and the people of all nations her friends. Far more to this gift of temperament than to those of her personal beauty or intellect, does she owe the eminence of her position among the American women of her century.

She was born early enough in the history of the Republic to partake in a measure of the glow of patriotic enthusiasm that had been the inspiration of its founders. Though she was intensely American, she grew up with no touch of bitterness for the mother-country, cherishing the memory of Chatham's words uttered in the House of Lords, "You cannot conquer America," rather than his sovereign's misguided efforts "to be a king."

Her grandfather, George Walton, who died two years before her birth, was one of the signers of the Declaration of Independence. He was a native of Prince Edward County, Virginia, but removed, prior to the Revolution, to Georgia, whence he was sent as a delegate to the first Congress. He had married, in the State of his adoption, Miss Camber, the daughter of an English nobleman and the heiress to large tracts of land that were grants from the crown. To this grandmother Octavia Walton was indebted for many graphic stories of the thrilling days through which her country had passed in establishing itself as an independent nation. She was in Philadelphia with her husband, who was in attendance upon the Congress there, when the news of the fall of Yorktown was received. The town was quietly sleeping when the watchman calling the hours announced, as usual, "Past midnight, and all's well!" then, after an instant's pause and in a voice that resounded through the streets, "And Cornwallis is taken!" It sent a thrill through the town, and turned that October night into day, for presently the streets were swarming with people wild with joyous excitement.

When Madame Le Vert related to Lamartine, with whom she passed an evening during one of her visits to Paris, in speaking of the Declaration of Independence, that her grandfather's name was thereon inscribed, and that he had given his blood and his fortune to the cause of America's freedom, the Frenchman arose and bowed to her profoundly. " Madame," he said, " in his name you have a noble heritage. It is the true patent of nobility, and you rightly cherish your descent from such a brave and heroic patriot with honest pride."

· The State of Georgia gave George Walton high honors, making him governor and, later, judge of the Supreme Court, and erecting a monument to commemorate his sterling qualities in one of the principal thoroughfares of the city of Augusta. His son and namesake married the accomplished and beautiful Miss Sally Walker, the daughter of a distinguished jurist of Georgia. Of the two children of their marriage,—a son and a daughter,—the latter was born at Bellevue, near Augusta, in the year 1810. She was named by her mother after the Roman Octavia, the beloved and noble sister of Augustus and the deserted wife of Marc Anthony, and was taught to revere the beauty of a character that possessed, as Pope Pius IX. said, when Madame Le Vert told him for whom she was named, " every virtue and grace that should adorn a woman."

Her early education was directed entirely by her mother and grandmother. An old Scotch tutor later assumed charge of the studies of Octavia and her

Octavia Walton
(Madame Le Vert)

brother, instructing them together in the sciences and languages. The facility with which Octavia mastered the latter was an evidence of the remarkable elasticity and adaptability of her nature. She acquired readily not only the language, but all the gestures and mannerisms of a foreign people. To her father this branch of her education was a matter of much interest. In the year 1821, when she was eleven years old, he became Secretary of State for Florida under Andrew Jackson, who was governor of the Territory. There often came to him in connection with the affairs of his office, letters and despatches in French and Spanish, of both of which languages she had so accurate a knowledge that he could entirely rely upon her translations of them. During a court ball at which she was present while in England, some years after her marriage, she delighted the ambassadors from France, Spain, and Italy by talking with each in his own tongue. She pleased the Holy Father no less upon the occasion of her audience with him, when, after he had spoken with her in both French and Spanish, thinking it might be less of an effort for him, she asked him to speak in his own tongue. During her residence in Florida, where her father succeeded General Jackson in the governorship, she also acquired a goodly store of Indian legends, which became later the delight of many an audience. She related on shipboard one night the story of Alabama having received the name from a tribe of Indians who were driven by a fierce northern foe to the forests of the southeast, and, coming upon a beautiful river, the chief struck his tent-pole, exclaiming "Alabama! Alabama!" meaning, "Here we rest." She was greeted, upon going on deck the following day, with an out-spread buffalo-robe, which a Chicagoan was taking to England as a gift for the Queen, and requested to make it her "Alabama" during the remainder of the voyage.

When her father selected a permanent seat of government for Florida, he permitted her to give it a name, and she called it Tallahassee,—the Indian word for "beautiful land,"—as a courtesy to the Seminole chief who had first pitched his tent on the spot. She had much sympathy and affection for the Indians, often pleading their cause against some act of aggression or injustice, and they had a tender reverence for her, calling her frequently "the white dove of peace."

One of the memorable events of her young life was the visit of Lafayette to America. It enters into the record of many lives that covered that period, some of which were far spent and some so tenderly youthful that the little marquis saluted them only by proxy, delegating somebody else "to kiss the babies" while he shook countless outstretched hands, for he was as complaisant as he was artistic. He wrote to the widow of his old friend, General George Walton, expressing a wish to see her during his stay in Mobile. Her health was not sufficiently robust, however, to admit of her undertaking a journey with the few comforts that were then possible. She sent her daughter-in-law and her granddaughter to represent her, intrusting to Octavia a miniature of her husband, the better to recall his features to Lafayette's memory and to enable him to realize how strong was the resemblance the little girl bore to her illustrious grandfather. She talked to him in French, so that the interview was to Lafayette a time of delightful relaxation, and it was with genuine reluctance that he saw it draw to a close. To Octavia it was the first in a long series of interesting memories associated with Mobile, whither her family removed from Florida in the year 1835. In the latter State, however, she spent the happy period of her young womanhood; hence Lady Emmeline Stuart Wortley, in some lines addressed to her at a later period, calls her "Sweet Rose of Florida."

Pensacola was the naval station of the gulf coast, and the constant coming and going of men-of-war, with the attendant festivities of balls of welcome and farewell banquets, were a distinctive feature in the social life of that portion of the Territory.

Octavia Walton, the governor's daughter, cultivated intellectually to a degree that made her the appreciative listener and intelligent talker among men of science and of letters, and with a personal beauty that made her the admiration of every one, occupied from her earliest girlhood a position of unusual prominence.

Long runs with her brother in the invigorating air of the coast had given to her supple figure, with its graceful curves, that erect carriage which she always retained. Her head was well poised, and her soft brown hair parted simply above a broad brow of unusual whiteness and transparency. In her blue eyes there lurked a suggestion of the cool and quiet depth of a forest, while her mouth, that feature which, says Oliver Wendell Holmes, we all make for ourselves, denoted the sweetness of her character. These were the visible forms of the loveliness of the young Octavia Walton, whom Frederika Bremer, the Swedish novelist, called "the magnolia flower of the South."

In 1835, the year her family moved to Mobile, accompanied by her mother and brother, she made a tour of the United States, visiting during the summer the famous resort of the North, Saratoga Springs, and going to Washington after the assembling of Congress in December. She attained a fame during that year that made her the inspiration of poets noted for the beauty of their lyric verse, and the subject of several analytical writings. She formed during the same period the friendship of two of the most eminent men of that time, Washington Irving and Henry Clay. She met Irving in travelling, and discovered his identity in a singular way. It was three years after his return from Spain, where he had represented his country with so much dignity and ability that his welcome home had been much in the nature of an ovation. The stage-coach, in which so many pleasant acquaintances were made, was yet the usual means of transportation, though the duration of journeys had been greatly lessened by the successful introduction of the steamboat, in which enterprise Fulton already had competitors, one young Vanderbilt running a rival line on the Sound between New York and Providence. Irving, who had been on the dock when Fulton made the first experiment with his steamer, used to relate with exquisite humor how the breathless silence of the crowd of curious spectators who watched her puff off into the stream was broken by the voice of an incredulous man saying, "She may go well enough for a time, but give me a good sloop." Being singularly shy, he usually talked but little among strangers. Divining in the young girl, who sat opposite him in the stage-coach for several days during the summer of 1835, those same qualities —"the sound and pure intellect and the heart full of affection"—that so endeared her to Miss Bremer, he dropped frequently into the current of bright talk she kept up with her mother and brother. They speculated frequently upon his identity, for his appearance was unusual, his manner courtly, and his language that of a most cultivated man. While she was talking with her brother in Spanish one day, he joined in their conversation and related some incident in connection with a bull-fight he had seen when in Spain. Octavia had already heard the identical story from another source, and, connecting the two narrations, she exclaimed, quickly, and quite unconsciously betraying the fact that his identity had been a matter of curiosity to her, "I know who you are! You are Washington Irving. Mr. Slidell, who related that story to me, told me that Washington Irving was standing beside him when it happened." Thus began a friendship that had an extensive influence upon her life. Realizing how keen were her powers of observation, and how unusual her command of language, he advised her to keep a journal, which was her first effort at writing, at which she attained later a leading position among women of letters at the South. He corresponded with her till the end of his life, and aided her with many suggestions gathered from his own experience in a long literary career. She in return shed many a ray of brightness over an existence that, with all its fame and success, was not without its lonely hours. The last time they met he reluctantly watched her departure from Sunnyside. "I feel, my child," he said, "that you are taking all the sunshine away with you."

Henry Clay looked upon her with the same tender pride that characterized Irving's attitude towards her. The beauty of her feet being at one time a subject of comment in his presence, he said that, while he was not prepared to pass judgment upon them, he was proud to be able to bear testimony to a beauty of tongue that he considered without parallel. Like Irving's, his friendship for her knew no change during the remainder of his lifetime. When the corner-stone of the monument erected to his memory in New Orleans was laid, she delivered an address that was well worthy of the eloquence of the man it eulogized.

In 1836 Octavia Walton was married, in the city of Mobile, to Dr. Henry S. Le Vert, a son of Dr. Claud Le Vert, who, coming to America as surgeon of the fleet under Rochambeau, had remained there after the termination of hostilities, settling in Virginia, and marrying a niece of Admiral Vernon. As Madame Le

Vert, Octavia Walton attained that same social sovereignty that was achieved a few years later by Mrs. Rush, of Philadelphia, and at a still more recent period by Mrs. Astor, of New York. The same sort of instinctive tribute was everywhere accorded each of these women, raising her to an eminence in which she was sustained by the unusual order of the gifts with which she was endowed. In Mobile, so absolute was the leadership of Madame Le Vert that she was frequently designated simply as "Madame," it being everywhere understood that the title without the accompaniment of any name applied only to her.

Her home on Government Street was the most noted of the city. There she entertained at various times not only the most distinguished of the people of her own country, but many eminent foreigners, Kossuth, among others, and Frederika Bremer. Lady Emmeline Stuart Wortley, the daughter of the Duke of Rutland, having been her guest for several weeks, gave her later that introduction that made possible the establishment of her social fame in England.

Joseph Jefferson, growing up in the profession in which he now stands in the foremost rank, and in whom she early recognized the divine spark of genius, had frequent proofs of the kindliness of her hospitality.

Her library was the feature of her home in which she always evinced the most interest. She never abandoned those habits of study which kept her in touch with the progressive minds of the world. Beauty alone is not sufficient to give a woman the place Madame

Le Vert filled. It attracts, but there must be behind it the sustaining force of an intelligence radiating sympathy, of a mentality developed and adorned with those graces that enable it to enter into and illuminate the lives that approach it. She continued to read in the foreign languages she had mastered in her early girlhood, painstakingly teaching them to her children, whom, in their infancy, she often sung to sleep with the love ditties of Italy. To her husband she was a continual source of revelation and pride. Precise, practical, profoundly interested in his profession, he felt little interest in the purely fashionable element of the life that revolved about her. In her relationship to it, however, her power to attract and hold such a diversity of tastes and temperaments he found an interesting study. At her levees and receptions it was his delight to take up his position where he could watch her, and, if possible, where he could occasionally catch the sparkle of her words.

To a nature keenly alive to every impression, the loss of her only brother, to whom she was attached by ties of an extraordinary sympathy, brought a grief that for a long time overshadowed her happy spirit. A few years after this loss,—in June, 1853,—accompanied by her father and the elder of her daughters, she made her first visit to the Old World, whose treasures and resources her classical education had so ably fitted her to enjoy. Her journal and letters written during this period and a subsequent trip ring with the enthusiasm of a girl. They formed the basis of her first published work, which met with much success, for in those days the theme was fresher, and she handled it with a a sprightliness that gave individuality and interest to every page. Very graphically she relates how the first ardor with which she embarked upon the new and delightful experience of a transatlantic voyage was quenched by that unromantic malady, sea-sickness. With the memory of the torture fresh upon her, she wrote that Solomon, when he ejaculated, " O that mine enemy would write a book !" probably knew nothing of the agonies of sea-sickness, or he would rather have invoked that malady upon him.

The London season was at its height when she arrived there. Well introduced, she created so favorable an impression upon a society where the success of an American depends largely if not entirely upon personal merit as evinced by his or her good breeding, intelligence, and powers to entertain, that she experienced all the delights of a hospitality which to the uninitiated is cold and exclusive. She was presented to the Queen at a court ball, to which she received the unusual honor of an invitation without a previous presentation to Her Majesty. With genuine regret she saw the days allotted to her stay in England draw to a close. Everywhere, however, she found and made friends, many strangers recognizing in her, in all its strength and purity, that sympathy which makes the world akin, and involuntarily opening their hearts to her. She was intensely interested in every one and everything, so that her life never contracted. Her early memories were associated with the Spanish, and she never outgrew her appreciation for the grace of their civilization. Her ability to speak the language added much to the pleasure and profit of her visit to Spain, and her journal recounting her stage-coach experiences contains frequent allusions to the unfailing courtesy of the people of that country. In Italy her knowledge of the language of the land again made her the spokesman of her little party, and with beneficial results. In Florence she had the pleasure of meeting the Brownings, and the interest they inspired in her seems to have been mutual. Mrs. Browning, whose health did not permit her to go out in the night air, broke the rule it had entailed upon her and went to a party given in honor of Madame Le Vert on the eve of her departure, that she might once more have the pleasure of seeing and talking with her. During one of her visits to Rome she had one of those peculiar experiences that evinced the friendliness she everywhere inspired. She had gone with her daughter to St. Peter's to attend the ceremony known as the Apostle's banquet. At the termination of the exercises there began an awful struggle for liberty in the packed isles of the great church. Madame Le Vert was well-nigh overpowered, when suddenly she felt herself lifted from her feet, raised high in the air, and safely ensconced on a window-ledge, while a reassuring voice whispered, in French, " There, little woman, don't be afraid ; you'll be safe there." Her rescuer was a powerful Russian woman, who, when she had placed Miss Le Vert beside her mother, said, simply, " Do not forget

me when you think of the Apostle's banquet," and
moved away with the surging crowd.

In all her journeys, both in her own country and in
Europe, she was accompanied by her colored maid
Betsey. "North, South, East, and West," wrote one
of her friends, "goes Betsey with her mistress through
bristling ranks of abolitionists, up the Rhine, over the
Alps, everywhere goes Betsey."

"If you would see the ideal relationship between a
lady and her female slave," said Frederika Bremer, "you
should see Octavia Le Vert and her clever, handsome,
mulatto attendant, Betsey. Betsey seems really not to
live for anything else than for her mistress Octavia."

At the Austrian border they were put through a series
of questions, all of their responses "being recorded,"
said Madame Le Vert, "for the benefit of posterity."
Betsey was put down as a Moor, much to her dismay,
and she besought her mistress to assure them that she
"had nothing but pure American blood in her veins,
and was a slave from the South."

During her second visit to Europe, in 1855, Madame
Le Vert spent the summer in Paris, the governor of
Alabama having named her Commissioner from that
State to the Paris Exposition of that year. His gallantry was a frequent subject of comment and appreciation, for she was the only woman among the commissioners. The position, however, seems to have been
purely honorary, for she lamented that when asked to
point out the products of Alabama in her department,
she could only indicate her daughter. "If there had

been even only a few cotton-seed," she said, " it would at least have served to swear by."

She witnessed the enthusiastic reception tendered by the French nation to the Queen of England, was present at the ball given by the Emperor in her honor, and was at the opera the night the royal party visited it, when the whole audience rose *en masse* at the first note of England's national anthem, sung by Roger, Alboni, and Cruvelli. She heard with a thrill of enthusiasm the " Vive la Reine Victoria" that burst from a thousand lips, and saw the Emperor lead the gracious queen three times to the front of the box to acknowledge the tumultuous tribute. In her own box sat, on that memorable night, an ex-President of the great republic across the water,—Millard Fillmore.

A visit made during her stay in Ferrara, Italy, to the home of the poet Ariosto so impressed Madame Le Vert that it was productive of a notable result after her return to America. His house had been purchased by the government, and everything in it was preserved in the order in which he had left it at the time of his death. Realizing that it was regarded as a shrine, and devoutly visited by those who would honor the memory of the immortal poet, her thoughts reverted to the home of the great American general, Mount Vernon, then falling into decay, whereas it might be similarly preserved by the patriotism of the people. She took up the question earnestly after her return to America, and did for the cause at the South as much as Mrs. Harrison Gray Otis did for it at the North. In one day she received at her home in Mobile, in small contributions, upward of a thousand dollars.

Many of Madame Le Vert's most charming letters were written to her mother. After a long day of travel or sight-seeing she frequently sat up far into the night that she might not neglect the pleasant duty of writing these letters.

Her parents' home in Mobile, of which city her father was for a time mayor, was near her own, and she continued to be much with them until their lives closed, which they did in close succession, shortly before the outbreak of the war. Her husband's death occurred during the last year of that melancholy period which shook the homes of the South to their foundation. She went North and remained for over a year after the close of the war, accompanied by her two daughters. She returned to the South for a time, but eventually removed to New York, disposing of her home and many of her possessions, the losses she had sustained and the altered conditions of her life rendering Mobile no longer to her a place of happy existence.

Having been so long a leader, she continued to exercise various queenly prerogatives, which to many people at the North seemed eccentric. She had not the prestige there that would have made them possible, though she was never without her coterie of admirers.

Her later years were not affluent, and she was obliged to put her talents to bread-winning purposes. She died in the city in which she had been born, Augusta, Georgia, on the 13th of March, 1877.

FANNY TAYLOR

(MRS. THOMAS HARDING ELLIS)

THE loveliness of Virginia women has been a theme of song and verse. Among the Richmond belles of sixty years ago none were more justly celebrated than that trio known as the Richmond Graces, Sally Chevalier, Fanny Taylor, and Sally Watson. Close companions from early childhood, their unusual beauty as they grew to womanhood brought them fame individually and collectively. Sally Chevalier became the wife of Abram Warwick, Sally Watson, of Alexander Rives, and Fanny Taylor, of whom this sketch is designed to treat at greater length, was twice married. She was educated at the excellent school of Miss Jane Mackenzie, in Richmond, at a time when a young lady's education embraced a rather superficial dip into the languages, a good deal of poetry, some history, a neat Italian handwriting, and a care of their peach-blossom complexions and slender hands. Frivolous as it sounds compared with the curriculum of girls' schools in good standing at this end of the century, the history of the South furnishes many evidences of the profundity as well as the brilliancy of its women.

Fanny Taylor
(Mrs. Thomas Harding Ellis)
From portrait by Thomas Sully

FANNY TAYLOR

With her friends, Sally Chevalier and Sally Watson, Fanny Taylor was a pupil in the dancing academies of Mr. Xaupi and Mr. Boisseau. They excelled in the grace and beauty of their dancing, and at the Assembly balls it was their custom to occupy places in the same cotillon. They enjoyed the delicate celebrity of having pieces of dancing-music named after them, and when "Sally Chevalier," "Fanny Taylor," or "Sally Watson," was called for, Judah, Ruffin, and Lomax, those dusky magnates of the ball-room, brought forth the melody with an air that was their own peculiar tribute to the fair young queens.

About the time she reached maturity, Fanny Taylor removed with her mother from Richmond to "Glenarron," the superb James River estate of her brother-in-law, Mr. William Galt. Shortly afterwards she returned to Richmond, where she spent a winter as the guest of her friends, Mr. and Mrs. Warwick. She became noted as the most beautiful woman in the Old Dominion. In a word, she was the belle of Richmond, which boasted the most delightful society in the South, and she would not have exchanged places with a princess of the royal house of England.

Richmond of those days was too small for social divisions and subdivisions. There was but one set, and every one who went into society at all belonged to it. It was well established and conservative. Its traditions were ancient, and it tolerated no innovations. It had its calling hours from twelve till four, when its drawing-rooms were crowded with young men from the neighboring plantations, professional men, and legislators, on whose ears the tones of the Capitol bell announcing the opening of the session were wont to fall in vain. There were dancing-parties for young people, beginning at seven or eight in the evening, and dinner-parties for distinguished guests at four o'clock in the afternoon.

The graceful art of carving formed an indispensable part of a gentleman's education, and a host gave tangible proof of his hospitality when from his end of the table he served his guests with his own hand, selecting the choice parts of a joint or fowl for the guest of honor.

The ladies retired at the conclusion of dinner, leaving the gentlemen in possession of the table, being a custom of their English forefathers which their colonial antecedents had adhered to probably in the log-cabin days when there was a state occasion.

There were no teas and no *débuts*. Girls never came out, because, as Thomas Nelson Page has said, "they had never been in." As soon as they were old enough to be out of the nursery they drifted naturally into the drawing-room, and there grew up in that social sphere which many of them were destined later to sway as queens.

Within a year after her reign in Richmond society Fanny Taylor became the wife of Archibald Morgan Harrison, of Fluvanna County, a most distinguished agriculturist, at a time when it was worth being a Virginia farmer and a country gentleman. They lived at "Carysbrook," Mr. Harrison's estate on the Rivanna

River, in the royal style easily possible to the South in her days of prosperity. She was a great-granddaughter of Benjamin Harrison, a signer of the Declaration of Independence, and her husband was a great-grandson of Benjamin Harrison, the father of Benjamin the signer. Their life of pastoral beauty closed with Mr. Harrison's death. His widow was at the height of her loveliness, and when she went once more into the world she evoked the most unstinted and genuine admiration. Mrs. Nellie Custis Lewis, who was expending on her motherless grandchildren all the solicitude that her grandmother, Martha Washington, had lavished upon her when she was similarly bereaved, expressed the desire that her son-in-law should woo Mrs. Harrison. So truly did she admire the qualities of her character, as well as her great personal beauty, that she was the only woman she had ever seen, she said, whom she would welcome as her daughter's successor, and willingly see placed over her grandchildren. She never had an opportunity to extend that magnanimous, however cordial, greeting, for the youthful Mrs. Harrison, after six years of widowhood, bestowed her hand upon Colonel Thomas Harding Ellis, of Richmond. He had been secretary of the American legation at Mexico, and was subsequently for nearly fourteen years president of the James River and Kanawha Canal Company, his administration covering the period of the war, when the canal was the most important line of improvement in the State for supplying with agricultural produce the city of Richmond and the army of Northern Virginia.

They visited Washington shortly after their marriage, where they were guests of Mr. John Y. Mason. Mr. Mason presented them to President and Mrs. Polk, whose courtesies to them added much to the pleasure of the Washington chapter of their honeymoon days.

Mrs. Ellis's mother had stood at the bedside of her uncle William Henry Harrison when, in the presence of his cabinet, he uttered those memorable last words, " I desire the principles of the Constitution to be maintained."

The union of Colonel and Mrs. Ellis terminated with the death of Mrs. Ellis in July, 1897, followed, in a few months, by that of her husband. For nearly fifty years had they traversed life's highlands and lowlands together, closest companions, tenderest of lovers, she possessing all the strength not incompatible with the finest and gentlest traits of female character, and retaining to the last all the delicacy of her wonderful beauty, and he the embodiment of chivalry, the highest type of a Virginia gentleman of the old *régime*.

Sally Chevalier
(Mrs. Abram Warwick)
By Thomas Sully

JESSIE BENTON

(MRS. JOHN C. FRÉMONT)

IN the year 1868 the city of St. Louis erected a
monument to the memory of one of her most distinguished citizens, Thomas Hart Benton. Of the
forty thousand people who thronged the park on that
May afternoon set aside for its unveiling, but one was
of the great man's blood, the daughter most closely
associated with the accomplishment of his loftiest conception, that dream of Western empire for his country.
Accompanied by her husband, General John C. Frémont, she had accepted the invitation to unveil the
statue. As she pulled the cord that loosened its wrap-
pings, and the school children of the city threw their
offerings of roses at the feet of him who had befriended
their fathers, the huzzas of the vast multitude filled the
fragrant air. The outgoing train to San Francisco
halted to salute with flags and whistles as the bronze
hand, pointing to the west, came into view, and the
words graven on the pedestal: "There is the East.
There lies the road to India." To General Frémont,
quietly and reverently occupying a place of honor on
the platform, it was one of those supreme moments
when the landmarks of memory, those events that give

color to our lives, stand forth to the exclusion even of
that which is at the moment passing before the eye.
Neither the vivas of the people nor the flowers of their
children thrilled him as did the salute of that out-
bound train, that thing of strength and power and
speed, bearing its message of progress and civilization.

He knew every mile of its route. He, the path-
finder, by his indomitable energy had traversed the vir-
gin snows of its mountain ways, had penetrated the mys-
teries of its wild valleys, and by his valor had given to
his country its golden terminus. And there, between
the effigy of the one in the radiance of the spring
sunshine and the living man, stood the woman
still radiant with that high type of beauty that emanates from the soul, the link, she has said of herself,
between the conception and the execution of the great
scheme of Western aggrandizement. Cradled among
great ideas, she had grown up to be an inspiration to
the man with the prowess and daring necessary to give
them life and form. Some men, such as Abraham
Lincoln, have been great in spite of their wives, while
to others, as to Frémont, through their wives have come
not only the opportunity for greatness, but with them
that identity of purpose that in itself is a fortification
against all adverse circumstances.

The story of Jessie Benton Frémont's life is closely
allied with that of the acquisition and development of
the vast territory west of St. Louis, which even in her
young womanhood was the outpost of habitation. Beyond its confines stretched that wonderland of her

childhood, whence came the trappers and hunters with their wild tales of adventure, and whither she was destined to follow one day the princely pied piper of her girlhood. The seed of the thought which bore its first fruit when Frémont raised our flag on Wind River Mountain, thirteen thousand feet above the Gulf of Mexico, was sown in the mind of her father when, in 1812, he followed Andrew Jackson from Nashville to New Orleans to defend the Mississippi. In the stirring life on its broad bosom, together with a first realization of the extent of our domain, he recognized the possibilities of our future expansion and greatness. He had already been admitted to the bar of Tennessee and was a member of the Legislature of that State. With the idea, however, that the government of the United States should extend its protecting arm over the great western wilderness, in which it evinced no interest and whence it anticipated no benefit, he moved, in his thirtieth year, to its border-land.

Its people recognized his friendly attitude, and when Missouri rose to the dignity of a representation on the floor of the United States Senate, Benton was the first man to whom she delegated that honor. There, for over thirty years, with a limited following, he fought aggressively foot by foot for the development of the West. He often wearied his hearers, who had but little sympathy with projects that to the remote Eastern mind seemed preposterous. It was not infrequently a signal, when Benton mounted his hobby, for his fellow-Senators to take up their letter-writing and for the galleries to be deserted. It made little difference to them if England's hand were outstretched and her fingers daily tightening their clutch upon our northwestern territory. The mouth of the Columbia River was about of as much consequence to the welfare of the United States, in the estimation of the people on the Atlantic seaboard, as are the canals on the planet Mars.

Commercial relations with Asia and ports on the Pacific, however Utopian they may have seemed to others with less of a grasp on the world's history than his scholarly mind possessed, were to Benton vital questions, for which he fought with that vigor of utterance that provoked John Randolph into saying that his family motto, " Factus non verbis," should be " Factus et verbis."

He was a powerful man, with a forcible way of speaking, which he retained to the end of his life. When he was stumping his State in the summer of 1856, being already in his seventieth year, he was cautiously viewed one morning through the crack of an open door by two anti-Bentonites. He was standing at the moment and speaking in a vigorous way that appalled his surreptitious visitors. " Good God," ejaculated one, " we shall have to fight him these twenty years !"

He was a striking figure, with heavy black hair and side whiskers, and during all the years that he was in the Senate, like some of his illustrious successors, he never changed the style of his dress. His vehemence was expended in public. In his family life he was as gentle as he was devoted.

Jessie, the second of his four daughters, and the subject of this sketch, was born at the home of her maternal grandfather, Colonel James McDowell, near Lexington, Virginia. She grew up partly in the picturesque atmosphere of St. Louis, then almost wholly a French settlement, and partly in Washington, where Benton's home was considered one of the most interesting in the city, owing to the cultivated wife and daughters who gave it character and individuality. Intermingled with her school-days she had her little day of belleship, during which the two most notable events were a dinner at the White House, given by President Van Buren for his young son, and the wedding of Baron Bodisco, the Russian minister, at which she appeared as first bridesmaid. The bride, Miss Williams, was one of her school-mates, and a girl of sixteen, while the bridegroom was over sixty. The details of the ceremony, however, were all harmoniously arranged by him, and included eight bridesmaids between the ages of thirteen and sixteen, and eight groomsmen of his own period of life. With one of the most distintinguished, James Buchanan,—then in the United States Senate, and but recently returned from the Russian mission,—walked Jessie Benton, fourteen years of age, and in her first long dress. Judged by his last will, this Russian January seems to have been an unselfish husband, for he therein expressed the wish that his still young wife should marry again and be as happy herself as she had made him.

The Van Buren dinner was a more or less memorable event, though the White House was familiar ground to Jessie Benton. During Jackson's administration she used frequently to go there with her father, for the old soldier-President was notably a lover of children. He liked to run his long fingers through her soft curls, while he talked with his old friend Benton, unwittingly giving the curls many a twist as he warmed to his subject, all of which the little girl bore heroically, finding ample recompense in her father's praise, which was sure to follow the ordeal.

She went to school both in St. Louis and Washington, in the former city principally for the sake of learning French by association with children to whom it was the mother-tongue. She spent two years at Miss English's boarding-school, in Georgetown, where she was not regarded as a diligent student. Many hours stolen from the class-rooms were not, perhaps, altogether unprofitably spent up a mulberry-tree listening to the fascinating accounts of a midshipman's life, as told by one of his cousins, and hanging hungrily upon every word, as if it in a measure foretold her own eventful career.

At home her mental training was continuous, and without conscious, or at least arduous, effort on her part. Each of Benton's daughters had her place at his library table, and there, stimulated by his studious habits, she acquired readily her portion of that vast fund of knowledge which he had gleaned first from his father's library of unusual excellence and later from his contact with men and measures of his day.

Of the measures there were many afoot when Benton's daughters were young, whose stupendous proportions we are scarcely able to gauge, knowing them only in the perfection of their full realization. Benton was the sympathetic friend of all progress, and beneath the steady glow of his astral lamp or the soft flicker of their mother's candles, in the nights before the advent of gas, his daughters, sewing each her fine seam, listened to the unfolding of the minds of the men who have developed America. They learned also those lessons of inexhaustible patience that must go hand in hand with every great undertaking and of the frequent subordination of the individual to the things his own mind has conceived.

Thither came Morse with that sublime faith in his conception of telegraphy that made him insensible or at least indifferent to the ridicule of Congress, where a member suggested, when he at length obtained his twenty-five thousand dollars for an experimental line to Baltimore, that a second appropriation should be made for an experimental line to the moon.

An overland emigrant route, the surveys for a railroad to the Pacific, and the Panama Railroad, Stevens coming to them directly from Central America and going later to the Isthmus, were some of the vast projects with whose details they were early familiarized. Later, when Jessie Benton, as Mrs. Frémont, crossed the Isthmus herself and was detained there by the fever, she saw Stevens every day, he coming, as he said, " to take his chill with her." He died in Panama, as he predicted that he would, one of the heroes in the vanguard of progress.

Into Benton's home quite naturally there drifted, in the year 1840, a young lieutenant of the corps of topographical engineers, fresh from the survey of the upper Mississippi. The son of a French father and a Virginia mother, John C. Frémont was born in South Carolina, in the year 1813. He was graduated, when he was seventeen years old, from Charleston College, where he remained to study civil engineering and teach mathematics. He was so unusually talented that Poinsett, the Secretary of War, recommended his services to Nicollet when the latter was about to undertake the survey of the Upper Mississippi. The two years in the field were followed by two years spent in Washington in preparing the scientific result of the expedition, during which period Benton became interested more perhaps in the work than in the individuality of the young officer, whose genius was later to open to us the western gates of our republic.

Accompanying Benton's eldest daughter to a concert at Miss English's school, Frémont for the first time met Jessie Benton. She produced on his mind at once " the effect that a rose of rare color or a beautiful picture would have done." She was but sixteen years old at the time, in the first bloom of girlish beauty, and her bright mind exhilarated by the pleasure of seeing her sister, poured itself forth in language as sparkling as it was natural. " Her beauty," he wrote later, in describing that first impression of her, " had come far enough down from English ancestry to be now in her that American kind which is made up largely of mind expressed in the face, but it still showed its Saxon descent. At that time of awakening mind, the qualities that made hers could only be seen in flitting shadows across the face or in the expression of incipient thought or unused and untried feeling."

Coming home for the Easter holidays, she found that the young lieutenant had become identified with her father's "Oregon work." He was an almost daily visitor at her home, and in his constant meetings with her in its unreserved atmosphere he found confirmation of the first impression he had formed of her. "There are features," he wrote later, "that convey to us a soul so white that they impress with instant pleasure, and of this kind were hers. Her qualities were all womanly, and education had curiously preserved the down of a modesty which was innate. There had been no experience of life to brush away the bloom."

Before the holidays were over this impression of her had penetrated Frémont's entire being, and he loved her no less profoundly than he admired her, rendering her an absolute devotion that knew no subsequent diminution. "Insensibly and imperceptibly," he said, "there came a glow into my heart which changed the current and color of daily life, and gave a beauty to common things."

That April day in 1841, when, a month after it had witnessed his inauguration, a mourning nation assembled to pay its last tribute to William Henry Harrison, a gray and gloomy day without, Frémont has recorded as the "red letter day" of his life. The government had leased quarters near the Capitol for the use of Nicollet, where the work on the map of the Mississippi's sources was going forward. From the windows of one of the rooms Senator Benton and his family were invited to view the funeral procession as it wound down Capitol Hill. Frémont, on leave of absence for the day, was the host of the occasion. Notwithstanding his best uniform, in which he looked very handsome, he personally tended the cheery log-fire, that gave a touch of cosiness to the big office, which he had, moreover, with somewhat reckless extravagance for a man on a lieutenant's salary, decorated with plants and cut flowers. From a daintily set table he served, with captivating grace, coffee and ices. Though the nation mourned, two hearts, at least, of all who looked upon the solemn pageant of that day were in gala attire.

The next day, though he discreetly sent Mrs. Benton the plants and flowers that had done decorative duty in his office, it availed him nothing in her wise eyes. Jessie was too young, and, besides, she did not wish her to marry an army man; the life was too unsettled. Mrs. Poinsett, the wife of the Secretary of War, was taken into her confidence, and, as a result, Frémont was ordered off to survey the Des Moines River. Jessie, moreover, as a further diversion, was taken to the wedding of one of her Virginia cousins, which meant in those days weeks of festivity.

It was but another case, however, of the best laid

plans that "gang aglee," for in the autumn both Frémont and Jesse Benton were back in Washington, and on the 19th of October she was courageous enough, in defiance of both father and mother, whom she not only loved but truly revered, to become Frémont's wife. She married too young, she says herself, ever to have been a belle in the usual acceptation of that term, yet so gifted has she been with those qualities that evoke the chivalry of man that but few American women have had a better right to that title. Though her life has been one of much exposure, she herself has at all times been singularly sheltered.

The year following his marriage, Frémont applied to the Secretary of War for permission to explore the far West and penetrate the Rockies. The plan was supported by Benton, who believed that by making surveys the government would be giving at least a semblance of protection to its Western possessions. Congress gave its sanction, and in May, 1842, with a handful of venturesome spirits gathered on the Missouri frontier, Frémont went forth to the exploration of the southern pass. It was the first of numerous similar expeditions, his scientific reports of which—going into astronomy, botany, mineralogy, geology, and geography—were translated into many tongues, and gave their author world-wide fame.

During his absences, which were always of uncertain duration, his wife sometimes remained in her parents' home. Her father sent for her one morning, when she had been married about a year, and, pointing out her old place at his library table, he said, " I want you to resume your place there; you are too young to fritter away your life without some useful pursuit." So she dropped back quite naturally into her old habits of study, as if her honeymoon days had been but another form of vacation.

She frequently accompanied Frémont, however, as far as St. Louis, waiting there for his return, or going out again to meet him after a fixed time. He was once eight months overdue, during which period of awful silence and suspense she had a supper-table set for him every night with all the comforts and luxuries of that civilization to which he had been so long a stranger. He came at length, in the dead of the night, and, rather than disturb a household, he went to a hotel, and for the first time in eighteen months slept in a bed.

With whatever misgivings she may have seen him set out for a field where he would encounter certainly many dangers, and possibly even death, she never, even when the opportunity came, of which many a weaker woman would have availed herself, endeavored to withhold him from his purpose. He would sometimes, after having covered many miles of his route, come back to her for another good-by, overtaking his party again by hard riding or pressing forward while they were resting.

In the summer of 1843, while he was still on the frontier gathering together men and animals for his second expedition, his recall to Washington was ordered, to explain there why, making a scientific expedition under the protection of the government, he had

armed his men with the howitzer. The order, however, never reached him, for he had already left St. Louis,
where it fell into the hands of his wife. Though she
still labored under the depression of their recent parting,
she yet, with all the spirit which the emergency demanded, sent him a swift messenger, bidding him hurry
off and rest and fatten his animals at Bent's Ford, stating
that there was sufficient reason for the haste which could
not then be given.

When he was quite beyond the reach of recall, for
it was before the days of telegraphy, she wrote to the
colonel of the Topographical Bureau, and confessed
what she had done, at the same time giving ample
reason for her action. To have obeyed the order, she
explained, would have meant the ruin of the expedition. Together with the time it would have required
to settle the party before he could leave it, the length
of the trip to Washington, and the inevitable delays
there, the early grass would be past its best, and the animals thus would be thrown underfed into the moun-
tains for the winter. She then replied to the charge
made against Frémont in the order of his recall. The
expedition must cross the country of the Blackfeet and
other unfriendly tribes of Indians, with no reverence
whatever for the cause of science, but with a very wholesome regard for any rights that were backed up with a
howitzer. Her father, who was absent from St. Louis
at the time, endorsed her action, and wrote to Washington, assuming the responsibility for it, saying he
would call for a court-martial on the point charged

against Frémont. Nothing further was heard of it, however, and the precious time, that meant so much more to the scientific mind of the explorer than to his government, to which all seasons are the same, was saved.

From an historical point of view this was the most important of all Frémont's expeditions. With the French territory which we had acquired by the Louisiana purchase we inherited also France's old feud with England, the underlying cause of which was the control of the markets in the East. When we took up the cudgels, their conflict, so far as the Western hemisphere was involved, had narrowed down to the ultimate possession of that portion of Mexico's territory which included the harbor of San Francisco. England had already made her survey of the ground, and her eye coveted that matchless port. She was the power we confronted in California when our war with Mexico ushered in the moment for decisive action. Two courageous, intensely American men, however, held the situation in their grasp,—in the Senate, at the climax of his powers, Benton, who had ever had a jealous eye upon England's encroachments on our boundary; in the field, Frémont, with all the gallantry and spirit that final coup demanded.

The British admiral, moving with more deliberation than the American colonel, with characteristic love of sport and appreciation of success, gracefully accepted his defeat, and tendered his felicitations to the intrepid rival, whose flag he found already floating above the coveted territory.

Frémont, after his gallant conquest, became the victim of a quarrel between two officers commanding the United States forces in that vicinity, and was brought back a prisoner over the territory he had acquired for his country. During the ninety days of his trial by court-martial, which stripped him of his commission as lieutenant-colonel of mounted riflemen, inspired by a lofty enthusiasm, his nights were devoted to writing the history of the expedition.

Though he was reinstated by the President, he returned his commission, and in 1848 took out a private expedition, opening the route from the Mississippi to San Francisco. His mountaineers flocked to him, ready to follow wherever he should lead. He had that faith in himself and in his purpose that evoked a corresponding confidence in them, and his presence was light and warmth and refreshment to their daring spirit. When it became necessary at times to divide the party, those who were not with him suffered sorely. The memorable winter of 1848, however, was one of hardships for all, travelling days and weeks within sight of eternal snows. Frémont wrote to his wife during a brief respite from that agonizing period, when his men were starving and freezing and wandering off in despair to lie down alone and die: "We shall yet enjoy quiet and happiness together; these are nearly one and the same to me now. I make frequent pleasant pictures of the happy home we are to have, and oftenest and among the pleasantest of all I see our library with its bright fire in the rainy, stormy days, and the large windows looking out upon the sea in the bright weather. I have it all planned in my mind."

Mrs. Frémont was, meanwhile, making ready for the long journey towards the land of this picture-home. It was the first break from the real home, her father's, where she had passed the greater part of the eight years of her married life, five of which her husband had spent in the field. She started in March, 1849, going by way of the Isthmus, where the man selected by Mr. Aspinwall for her guide had many misgivings about undertaking the charge. He had a wife, who had prophesied that, coming from Washington, Mrs. Frémont would be " a fine lady" and would make him no end of trouble, especially concerning the scant attire of the Indians.

In the sunshine of her presence, however, his misgivings melted away. She was not a " fine lady" at all, he said, that bugbear of his unconventional mind, but a slender woman with a head so level and a heart so stout as to render all the more forcible the appeal of her delicate body.

She was stricken with the fever, and ill for many weeks in Panama, where she was surrounded with that warmth of friendship and sympathy which she ever seemed to attract. In addition to many substantial evidences of genuine interest in her recovery, one resident of the city vowed in that event to supply the hospital with limes for a year.

Gold was discovered in California in 1848 When Mrs. Frémont arrived in San Francisco the people were in that first frenzy of excitement that disturbed temporarily the whole aspect of their daily existence. The population of the towns was flocking to the mines, and the comparatively few who remained at home had many novel problems to face. The art of cooking without eggs and butter had to be acquired, for there were neither chickens nor cows, though one woman had as many as thirty-seven satin dresses, " and no two off the same piece," she averred.

A little Eastern bride, whom San Francisco society, consisting of sixteen ladies, turned out in a body to welcome, set up her first household belongings in a modest frame structure two stories in height, that had been put up at a cost, out of all proportion to its intrinsic value, of ninety thousand dollars.

Yet nothing was so valuable as time, and though it was estimated to be worth fifty dollars a minute, there were busy men who paid Mrs. Frémont the compliment of frequent day-time visits

With every personal inducement to favor slave labor in the new territory, both Frémont and his wife were among its most strenuous opposers. Not only did they pay their first house-maid two hundred and forty dollars a month with perquisites, which included the housing of her husband and children, yet even with a disposition to retain her at that neat figure, they found themselves obliged to do without her truly valuable assistance when Mrs. Frémont refused the loan of her gowns as patterns for the wardrobe she was having constructed at the hands of a Chinese modiste. There were, moreover, on the lands that Frémont owned, rich gold deposits, which could be most profitably operated by slave labor.

When the convention to draft the constitution under which California should come into the Union met at Monterey, where Frémont had established himself, his home became the head-quarters for the anti-slavery party. Its neatness, the smoothness of its internal workings, and the evident contentment of his wife formed a text for the friends of free soil, and many an incredulous opponent was brought to behold, and, seeing, went away believing in the possibility of domestic happiness without slaves. Mrs. Frémont had, to be sure, a preference for underclothing that had been ironed, and she might have wished also that the two Indian men who presided in her kitchen and pantry had not been gifted with such facilities for terminating both the ornamental and useful career of her china and glassware. Yet these small clouds in no way overshadowed her domestic horizon. Her prejudice to slavery she inherited from both parents, belonging, as she said, " to the aristocracy of emancipation," or to that class of people who, owning slaves, quietly gave them their freedom at infinite sacrifice to themselves, as opposed to the abolitionists of the North, who, with nothing to lose and much to gain, clamored noisily for that freedom.

Frémont was the hero of the hour, and could have been governor of the new State or one of its first Senators. He chose the latter, however, though it took him away from those material interests which California then held for him. Going into the Union as a free State, it would need in Congress a defence such as no man could give it with greater loyalty than Frémont.

There is an anecdote told and applied indiscriminately to various political heroes, most frequently, perhaps, to Lincoln, to whom, therefore, it may possibly appertain, demonstrating delicately his deference for the marital tie. On the night of his election to some office, and while he was being inundated with the congratulations of the friends who had assisted in the achievement of his triumph, he further captivated their fancy by remembering his wife. "Well, gentlemen," he said, quietly, "this is very nice, but there is a little woman around the corner who will be interested in hearing this news, and if you will just excuse me, I think I'll step around and tell her."

One woman interested in the balloting of the delegates at San José for California's first Senators was not so conveniently situated. She was at Monterey, and as a season of heavy rains was on, there was but little prospect that her keen desire to know the result would find immediate gratification. Before just such a merry blazing fire as his imagination had once conjured up as a central feature of their library sat Frémont's wife, her fingers for the first time fashioning a dress for herself on the trustworthy outlines of one that had been ripped up for the purpose. Her little daughter had been put to bed, and her companions for the evening were the Australian woman who had replaced her two Indian servitors, and whose accustomed fingers plied the needle with a more rapid stroke than her own, and the woman's baby, playing on the bear-skin rug near the fire. Besides the voice of the woman and an occasional chirrup from the baby, she heard nothing but the storm without, till the door opened and a man, dripping with rain, stood on the threshold and asked, in consideration of his sorry plight, if he might enter.

It was Frémont. He had torn himself away from his idolizing followers and ridden out into the darkness and storm to tell his wife, seventy miles away, that he had been elected to the United States Senate. Though it was late in the night when he reached Monterey, he was in the saddle again before dawn and on his way back to San José, making in all a ride of one hundred and forty miles.

The home-bound steamer, sailing from San Francisco on the 1st of January, 1850, carried, among others, the first two Senators from the new State, Frémont and Givin. At Mazatlan a British man-of-war fired a salute in honor of these two distinguished passengers.

They landed in New York the last of March, and from the long mirror into which she looked, in her hotel bedroom, there gazed back at Mrs. Frémont a comely young woman clad in a riding habit that had been abbreviated to a convenient walking length, a pair of black satin slippers, a leghorn hat tied down with a China crêpe scarf, and a Scotch plaid shawl that had borne the brunt of her year's outing,—in a word, the wife of a United States Senator from the golden West.

On another morning of the early spring two years

later, such were the contrasts which the events of her
life produced, she stood in the throne-room of Buckingham Palace, awaiting presentation to the Queen of
England. To the British eyes that looked upon her
she was a graceful, distinguished woman, sharing in the
renown of her husband, the American explorer, and a
recent medallist of the Royal Geographical Society,
whose honors are only conferred upon those whose
expeditions are taken out at personal cost and sacrifice.
In the faultless details of her court dress she was a
gratification to the most critical taste. Its exquisite
design, shading in color from the faint pink that touches
the outer edge of a rose petal to the deeper tone it
assumes near the heart, with clusters of the fair flower
itself giving it an almost fragrant emphasis and bringing out the delicate beauty of her fine face, seemed a
part of herself, so gracefully did she wear it, carrying its
sweep of train with a queenliness that was of her nature.

On the 17th of June, 1856, Frémont was unanimously nominated for the Presidency by the National
Republican Convention at Philadelphia. He was the
first choice of the Free Soil, which became, later, the
Republican party, and he was also, probably, the only
man of whom Lincoln, the first successful candidate of
that party, was ever jealous. Fearing a military rival,
and recognizing in Frémont the qualities that gave him
a natural supremacy among men, he kept him in the
background. He foresaw correctly. The military hero
came, but he came in the person of the man to whom
opportunity had been a fairy god-mother.

Though he polled the vote of all the Northern States but five, the time was not ripe for a Republican President when Frëmont was a candidate for that high honor. The men, like Benton, who still led the political thought of that day, and who knew every aspect of the country, realizing the peril that lay in countenancing sectionalism, could not give their support to a candidate who stood upon a sectional platform.

Whatever were his hopes or his disappointment, his wife shared them. His accepting the nomination from so radical a party had meant the breaking up of many friendships for her, which in itself was a genuine grief to a woman of her temperament. The anguish she endured during the first months of the war between the North and the South, which she spent in St. Louis among familiar faces, whom the circumstances of her position as the wife of a Northern general had estranged from her, left its record in her beautiful hair, which, from a warm brown, became quite white within a few weeks. No matter with what heroism we endure, we sometimes bear all the rest of our lives the scars which our courage has cost us.

She has never outgrown, however, her early attachment to the South, to which she is united by many ties of blood. During the famine there that followed the war she applied to Congress for relief, which was immediately granted, with a ship to carry all the supplies the Freedman's Bureau could furnish. With warm and tender sympathies she has always taken up any cause that appealed to her with an enthusiasm that communi-

cated itself to others. Relating to Mrs. Dix one evening the case of one of Lieutenant Frémont's men, who
had been disabled by being wounded in both legs, and
to whom Congress had refused a pension on the ground
that he had not been regularly enlisted at the time the
wound was inflicted, she did not observe that a man
who was calling upon Senator Dix was attentively listening to all the graphic details of her story. It was
Preston King, of New York, and at that time chairman of the Committee on Appropriations. He took
Senator Dix to the door with him when he left, and
bade him tell her to write out the story as she had just
told it and send it to him, and he would see that the
man got his pension ; and he did.

With what tender gratitude and reverence the man
himself, Alexis Ayot, a Canadian by birth, came to
thank her !

" I cannot kneel to thank you," he said, balancing
himself upon his crutches, " Je n'ai plus de jambes ;
but you are my Sainte Madonne, et je vous fais ma
prière."

During her early California days she extended her
generous young hand to a youthful compositor who
was working on the *Golden Era*. He dined with
her every Sunday, and she gave him not only that
recognition and encouragement that were in themselves
a stimulus to his talent and ambition, but she used her
influence to obtain for him salaried offices that lifted
him above anxiety concerning his material condition,
and gave him the leisure necessary to the best devel-

opment of his genius. His name is Bret Harte, and so entirely did he recognize his indebtedness to her that he once wrote to her : " If I were to be cast away on a desert island, I should expect a savage to come forward with a three-cornered note from you to tell me that at your request I had been appointed governor of the island at a salary of two thousand four hundred dollars."

She has both the versatility and adaptiveness that are characteristic of the genuine American woman, and which have enabled her to make almost as many friends in foreign lands as she has throughout her own country. The Count de la Garde, a cousin of Eugene and Hortense Beauharnais, whom she knew in Paris, and who left her at his death a valuable collection of souvenirs of the Bonaparte family, said of her that she was the only American woman he had ever known. He had known others of her countrywomen, but they were but imitations of English or French women, while in her he felt the originality and individuality of another people.

As a scientist and explorer, Frémont's reputation had gone forth to the countries of Europe, from many of which he received enviable honors and decorations. He and his wife were presented at the courts of England, France, and Denmark, attending at Copenhagen the wedding-festivities of the Crown Prince and his Swedish bride. As one of her friends has cleverly said of Mrs. Frémont, " she has entertained and been entertained through not only the gamut but the chromatic scale of society."

JESSIE BENTON

After the war, while her younger children were still growing up, and during her husband's lifetime, she lived for some years in New York, on a picturesque old property on the Hudson that still bore its Indian name, Pocaho. Now, however, she lives again in the State that once gave her health, wealth, and honors, near the great sea, away from which she feels that she is never fully alive.

Her life has been full of changes and events, to all of which her alert intelligence and quick sympathies have made her keenly susceptible, and which wrung from her recently a plaintive, " We are tired, my heart and I." That was all, for one who knew every phase of her life has already borne testimony to that " sweet and happy and forbearing temper which has remained proof against the wearing of time."

SALLIE WARD

(MRS. GEORGE F. DOWNS)

ONE of those extraordinary women which the world from time to time produces, who rise to eminence solely through the force of their own personality, was born in America as the nineteenth century was rounding out its first quarter. Known all her life throughout the entire country, she was one of the most conspicuous figures in the life of the South and Southwest, and was the object of a sentiment that fell but little short of worship among the people of the state of Kentucky, to which she belonged.

James Lane Allen who has studied his people from every stand-point, draws the typical Kentucky woman for us as "a refinement of the English blonde, with greater delicacy of form, feature, and color."

"A beautiful Kentucky woman," he says, "is apt to be exceedingly beautiful. Her voice is almost uniformly low and soft, her hands and feet delicately formed, her skin quite pure and beautiful in tint and shading, her eyes blue or brown, her hair nut-brown or golden; to all which is added a certain unapproachable refinement."

Of such a class, Sallie Ward, with her blue eyes full

of twinkling humor and rather far apart, lending to her round face an expression of candor, which was further borne out by her somewhat large though finely shaped mouth disclosing handsome teeth in her happy tendency to frequent smiling, her brown hair, and a skin faultless in tint and texture, has been the most noted representative. A radiant woman, instinct with sparkling life from the crown of her beautiful head to the tips of her slender feet, spoiled, wilful, lovely, and loving, it is probable that but few people will ever truly estimate her character.

She was the daughter of Robert J. Ward, a man of considerable wealth and of that distinction of manner and bearing which is commonly designated as of the old school. Like many another gifted young Kentuckian, similarly placed in life, he began his career with political aspirations, and before he had reached his thirtieth year he had been elected Speaker of the State Assembly. His own private concerns, however, gradually absorbing his time and interest, drew him away from his youthful ambitions. He married the heiress of a large fortune, Miss Flournoy, of Georgetown, Kentucky, the descendant of an old Huguenot family, to whose fame her immediate ancestors had further contributed by the gallant part they had taken in the war of the American Revolution.

Sallie Ward, one of the eldest of a large family of children, was born on her grandfather's estate in Scott County. She went to boarding-school in Philadelphia, the reputation of whose educational institutions in the first half of the century surpassed those of any other city in the country. At even an earlier period, an entry in the journal of Charles Carroll of Carrollton, one of the most enlightened men of his age, shows in what high estimation they were held, from the fact that he mentions no other, though the praise in this instance is rather of a negative order. He records in 1816 that he has sent his little granddaughter, Mary Harper, to a school in Poitiers under the care of Mr. Gallatin, then our minister to France, "where she will be more piously educated than in the very best boarding-school in Philadelphia."

There were some good students, no doubt, to uphold the reputation of well-established schools, though it was before the influence of Hannah Adams, the pioneer of a broader education for women, had been widely felt, and before that delicate balance between the mental and physical being of a girl student had ever been disturbed by over-study. With that "little learning," that was not "a dangerous thing" from the point of view of the women of that day, there were many with a mental sprightliness that was far more exhilarating than all their deep draughts from the Pierian spring had rendered a few such women as Hannah Adams. A disappointed man who once made a stage-coach journey with her related that she only opened her lips to enumerate the pieces of baggage with which she was encumbered, lest in her descent she should, in the preoccupation of her mind, leave behind her either her "great box, little box, or bandbox."

Sallie Ward
(Mrs. George F. Downs)
From a miniature

SALLIE WARD

Sallie Ward, in deference perhaps to the prejudices of her French origin, was sent to a school presided over by a woman of that nationality. She enlivened its atmosphere of conventional elegance by many startling ebullitions of her undisciplined young spirits, such as appearing unannounced in male attire at wholly inappropriate moments. Then, as everybody disappeared with more haste than dignity, her own uncontrollable laughter would reveal the truth of the situation. Some one would exclaim, " Sallie Ward!" and the others would troop back to admire her, for, if a little effeminate, she made, nevertheless, a very captivating youth, and no school-mistress could ever look into her beaming face and find it in her heart to be harsh to her.

Her own mother attempted once when she was a very little child to punish her for some misdemeanor, but Sallie, divining her purpose, dropped quickly on her knees and raised her little hands in supplication. There seemed at that moment something so seraphic in her childish beauty that her mother afterwards admitted that her good intentions were involuntarily thwarted. Though the rod was always spared, she grew up to be none the less lovable, though a woman of the world in all things rather than a woman of the spirit,—the logical result of her environment.

A subtle quality that goes forth from some personalities, commanding instant attention and reverence, went forth from Sallie Ward, evoking everywhere admiration and love. She realized the power herself, and it enabled her to do everything with an indefinable grace proceeding from an absolute self-confidence. That which would have seemed daring coming from another woman was approved and applauded in Sallie Ward. She possessed a knowledge of horses that is more or less common among the women of Kentucky, and rode with a dash and skill which the women of no other State have ever surpassed. She sometimes capriciously utilized this accomplishment to test a man's devotion, doing apparently without premeditation some daring feat and discovering thereby the extent to which he would follow her, for every man was at least worth measuring weapons with, though in the process she unwittingly, no doubt, despoiled many a less dazzling woman. She was, however, only exercising what she conceived to be the prerogative of every woman. While riding in Louisville one day she came upon the market-house, which ran for some distance through the centre of the street. Instead of going around it, she impulsively dashed through it without in any degree slackening her speed. The man who was with her unhesitatingly followed, and was rewarded, as he drew up beside her on emerging from the far end of the structure, with an arch smile and "Now, sir, you'll have a pretty fine to pay, twenty-five dollars apiece, for that little stretch." When he went the next day, however, to pay the penalty for the pretty caprice, he found that the obligation had already been quietly discharged by Miss Ward herself.

She had innumerable lovers and suitors all her life, and never, even in its closing years, entered any assemblage, small or great, private or public, that her name did not pass from mouth to mouth till all were aware of her presence. She was the glorious heroine of many a shy girl's first ball, while the forlorn little maid whom it purported to introduce to the social world clung timidly to the wall, with admiring eyes, however paradoxical it may seem, upon the radiant being who with apparent unconsciousness was carrying off all the honors of the occasion. The remarkable popularity of Sallie Ward has been compared to that of a feudal princess in her hereditary domain. It was confined to no class, but entered into all grades of society, parents in all walks of life naming their children after her, and children in turn naming their pets after her. Many a product of the far-famed stock-farms of the blue-grass State was likewise honored with a name that came to be a synonyme for all excellence. "It is a perfect Sallie Ward," or, "I've a regular Sallie Ward," was the proud boast of many a man who owned anything whatsoever that he esteemed of superlative quality.

A mother once putting her little girl to bed related to her as a lullaby the story of the creation of the world, pointing out its beauties and blessings as they came from the hand of God.

"He made the sun that shines in the day," said the mother, "and the moon and the stars that we see in the night, and all the flowers that beautify the world, and the birds that gladden it with their sweet song."

"And mother, don't forget," interrupted the child. He made Sallie Ward, too."

When the governor of Kentucky, at the outbreak

of the Mexican War, was called upon to furnish a regiment of infantry, both the Louisville Legion and the Louisville Guard, among whose officers and men were enrolled many names of which the State was justly proud, volunteered for service. Sallie Ward was selected to present the flags to both companies, and the enthusiasm of the people, when on the bright May morning of their departure the Legion passed in review before her home, testified to the concurrence of the entire city in the choice. There was a prolonged shout of rapture from the throng of spectators as many eyes dim with weeping beheld the already familiar form of Sallie Ward standing beneath the silken folds of her country's flag. Their cheers redoubled as she presented it to the standard-bearer, and they continued to ring in her ears as she waved her own farewell to the embryo heroes, many of whom carried away that last picture of her standing in the sunshine of that bright morning to be an inspiration in a darker hour. She drove to Portland to present the flag to the Guards, who embarked from that point. As they marched by the open carriage in which she sat at the conclusion of the ceremony of the presentation, every man saluted her, and she afterwards declared that it was the proudest moment in a life of many triumphs.

Her father's wealth not only enabled him to maintain one of the most elaborate establishments in Louisville, but in the summer to transport his numerous family, accompanied by men- and maid-servants, in travelling-carriages to the White Sulphur Springs, where

his daughters were successively belles. A portion of
each winter, including the season of the Mardi Gras,
was spent in New Orleans, for though the facilities for
travelling that exist to-day were not known at that
time, a man blessed with the worldly goods that Mr.
Ward possessed could not only permit his family to
make frequent journeys, but to make them also under
most comfortable and agreeable circumstances.

In this way the fame of Sallie Ward was well established at the South when, before she had reached her
twentieth year, she married Bigelow Lawrence, of Boston, and entered upon her brief career at the North.
The man who thus won her from many Southern
rivals was many years her senior, and it was to a
woman of her temperament a most unfortunate alliance. He was the son of the Hon. Abbott Lawrence, who had been our minister to England, and
was himself a man of wealth and distinction and an
exquisite gentleman of the severe Boston school, whose
ethics were wholly at variance with that spirit of
liberality which was all Sallie Ward had hitherto known.
Developed in an atmosphere of almost passionate admiration, love and appreciation had become as necessary to her being as light and air. Transplanted in the
very effulgence of her bloom to a frigid temperature of
critical and unsympathetic surroundings, all her spontaneous grace congealed into acts of deliberate effron-
tery. Bewildered by a chill she had never before felt,
too young and inexperienced in the ways of the world
beyond those of her own genial climate, where she had

been a law unto herself, to realize aught of the value of mutual concessions, she struck blindly against the cold conventionality in which she felt herself encaged. It was a strange and almost cruel fate that put her in the bosom of the Lawrence family, and occasioned as much suffering to her Southern heart as to their Northern sensibilities.

At a ball given in Boston about the time Mrs. Bloomer was seeking to introduce her reform in woman's dress, and while the subject was being widely discussed. Sallie Ward, then the wife of Bigelow Lawrence, appeared in a costume designed on the Bloomer pattern. Socially conservative Boston was agog, and Lawrence achieved through his wife an unenviable notoriety. Another of her proclivities wrought additional sensation and consequently further havoc in his social status. Notwithstanding the natural beauty of her complexion, it was whispered even in Louisville that she sought with more or less artistic skill to further embellish it. One day when the artifice was unusually apparent, as she passed a group of laboring men, one exclaimed, audibly, "By God, painted!" Nothing daunted and without changing color, the story runs, she said, quietly, "Yes, painted by God," and passed on.

Her mother, realizing the unhappy condition of her life with Mr. Lawrence, took her home, and within a year she applied to the Legislature of Kentucky for a divorce, which was granted on the ground of incompatibility of temper. She took her maiden name and lived for several years in retirement.

SALLIE WARD

Her first reappearance in that world of gayety and social emulation which was her natural element was at a ball given in Louisville, and where at midnight, though everybody knew she was in the house, she had not yet made her appearance. Shortly after twelve o'clock the music suddenly ceased; in an instant silence fell upon the ball-room; some one whispered " Sallie Ward," and every one pressed towards the stairway. She was, indeed, a vision of radiant loveliness that held every man and woman spellbound as she descended its winding length. She was enveloped in white tulle, which seemed to float about her like a cloud, a jewelled pin catching the meshes of a filmy veil and holding it imprisoned in her brown hair. One arm covered with jewelled bracelets was extended, the hand resting in that of the man who had the honor of leading her. So light and floating was the effect she produced that the tips of her white slippers seemed scarcely to touch the steps.

She was at all times supreme and irresistible without resorting to extraordinary effects, which she frequently did, for she was not lacking in that vanity which is " the cordial drop," said John Adams, " that makes the bitter cup of life go down," though an existence filled with so many sweets as was hers could have needed no such stimulus.

At a fancy-dress ball given in her honor at Lexington, she created an unparalleled sensation by changing her costume four times in the course of the evening, reaching the climax as an houri.

Her second marriage was to Dr. Hunt, of New Orleans, where she was already well known. The city, with its contingent of wealthy Spanish and French planters, contained many homes whose palatial splendors exceeded those of the most pretentious establishments of other localities. The new home in which Sallie Ward came to preside was on a scale of magnificence that fully gratified her luxurious tastes and love of the beautiful. Its rich adornment of tapestries, statuary, and Parisian furnishings, its marble court, with its glistening fountains and wealth of tropical bloom, formed an exquisite background for her artistic individuality and prodigal temperament. Its hospitalities were munificent and the legend of the magnificence of its dinner-parties, during which the orchestra from the French opera filled the court-yard and dining-room with its melodies, was the marvel of a people accustomed to entertaining with all the luxurious accompaniments of a most artistic civilization; and into all of whose forms of a ceremonious existence there entered a perfect harmony that was a second nature to them.

The years of her residence in New Orleans represent the most brilliant period of Sallie Ward's life, when her surroundings, combined with her natural gifts, gave her easily that leading position which she filled so graciously and with so much happiness to herself. Her only child, Mr. John Hunt, of New York, was born of this marriage.

After her husband's death she returned to Louisville, and there for some years devoted herself to rearing and educating her son. She was subsequently twice married, the first time, after nearly fifteen years of widowhood, to Mr. Vene P. Armstrong, and the second time to Mr, George F. Downs, both of Kentucky. She retained till the end of her life, which closed in the summer of 1898, all her remarkable powers of attraction.

Surrounded always with the pomp and vanity of life, and deeply imbued with the maxims of a worldly philosophy, she yet preserved intact an unselfish heart that not only prompted her to many deeds of noble philanthropy, but to countless little acts of kindness graciously performed that beautified lives less fortunate than her own. With her quick bright mind and gift for clever repartee, she sent many a ripple of irresistible drollery over the current of the life that encircled her, and sped many a shaft of stinging wit into the armor of a hollow conventionality. "How lovely of you to say that! but then you always say such sweet things of everybody," was the meaningless flattery in the response of a woman to whom she had spoken in heartfelt praise of another woman. "Did you ever hear, madam," retorted Mrs. Downs, "that I had said anything sweet of you?"

She never could have attracted and held the universal homage that was undoubtedly hers had there not radiated from her a power quite beyond that bestowed by the material possessions of the world,— the potency of a vivid and lovable personality. Had she been a man, she would have been capable of such acts of gallantry and daring as characterized "mad" Anthony Wayne or General Custer. As she was a woman, with her field restricted to the social world, from whose stand-point she must necessarily, therefore, be judged, her singular genius was productive of many extraordinary achievements, through all of which there was a very audible appeal for the love that never failed her, but which was given to her in such measure as perhaps to no other woman ever born in America.

HARRIET LANE

(MRS. HENRY ELLIOTT JOHNSTON)

OF the men who have filled the Presidential chair of the United States, about none as about James Buchanan has romance hung that halo which in his case tends but to throw into bolder relief the substantial side of his character. Men of more dash, of more picturesque individuality have filled that high office than was he who rose to it through the gradations of a long legislative career.

When he entered Congress, though he was but twenty-nine years old, the chapter of sentiment had already closed for him, and it was never reopened during a long life, the greater part of which was passed in the gaze of a scrutinizing public. This fact alone is sufficient to render him unique in the estimation of a people who have a primitive love for the story where all ends happily.

There was nothing in Buchanan's appearance nor in his attitude towards life in general that suggested the tragic episode of his youth. It is only in retrospect that we realize the glamour it cast over his subsequent years. Nature reacts through various channels, and in him she sought her outlet in an unabating mental activity. He was a student all his life.

To the world he was a man of somewhat grave appearance, a typical anglo-saxon, immaculate in his dress, conservative in his speech, and yet with a grace and dignity of manner that added much to the distinction with which he represented his country at the court of Russia in 1832, and again twenty-one years later at the court of St. James.

His attitude towards women was that of chivalric regard, and the close relationship he bore to one of the most beautiful women of her period, being both her uncle and guardian, displays one of the most interesting sides of his character. Much of the charm that attaches to the history of the more conspicuous years of his public career emanates from Harriet Lane. No woman has ever presided in the White House who roused so universal an interest, unless it was Mrs. Cleveland, as did Buchanan's niece.

Her countrymen honored her in every conceivable way, and her name was a household word. Vessels of war and of peace bore it to foreign shores. Clubs, streets, houses, and even articles of dress were named after her.

There was a majestic isolation about both Harriet Lane and James Buchanan. Death had stripped them both,—Buchanan in his youth of the woman who might have rounded out his life, and Harriet Lane, one by one, of mother, father, sister, and brothers. She came into the White House bearing the burden of personal loss in the recent death of her only sister. As she came out of it the travail of coming war had already cast its shadow upon the nation.

Yet, socially, the White House was never so brilliant as it was during the administration of Buchanan. "The White House," said Jefferson Davis, referring later to his last days in Washington, "under the administration of Buchanan approached more nearly to my idea of a republican court than the President's house had ever done before, or since the days of Washington."

A picture that the people seemed never to tire of looking upon was of the grave bachelor-President with his beautiful niece beside him doing the honors of the nation. She was at the climax of her glorious womanhood during the period she passed in the White House. Contact with the world, together with her recent touch of sorrow, had worn away the angles of her youthful exuberance. She had attained a golden maturity, and with a perfection of physical development she united a dignity and a confidence in herself restful to behold. "Every motion," Mary Clemmer wrote of her at that time, "was instinct with life, health, and intelligence. Her head and features were cast in noble mould, and her form, which at rest had something of the massive majesty of a marble pillar, in motion was instinct alike with power and grace."

She had a warmth of coloring that further bore out the idea of abundant health. Her hair was of a golden-brown hue, and worn always with that absolute simplicity which best became her well-shaped head. Her eyes were of a deep violet and her mouth was faultlessly beautiful, with its full red lips and upward curve.

She was as discreet, said one of her admiring critics, as she was beautiful, and her uncle's confidence in her was without bounds. Even as a little child, when falling far short in many respects of his somewhat austere ideals of propriety, she had inspired in him a reverence for her absolute truthfulness. " She never told a lie," he once said, in speaking of her childhood ; " she had a soul above deceit or fraud. She was too proud for it."

She came into Buchanan's life like a breath of wind from the mountain-side, fresh, sweet, and wild. Buchanan was distraught. His bachelor habitat was in confusion. He was a man of theories and ideals. This bit of youthful life that had elected to invade the quiet of his days was a being of impulse, however generous, of exuberant health and spirits. A sense of his superiority, however, penetrating her youthful intelligence, gave him that influence over her that was productive of such satisfactory results as she grew to womanhood.

Through her father, Elliot Lane, whose family had emigrated to Virginia during the war of the American Revolution, she was of English descent. From the north of Ireland, about the same time, also had come her maternal grandfather, James Buchanan. He married Elizabeth Spear, the daughter of a farmer, and settled in Franklin County, Pennsylvania, then and for some years later central ground and the great highway between the East and the West. James Buchanan, afterwards President of his country, and Jane, the

Harriet Lane
(Mrs. Henry Elliott Johnston)
From photograph by Julius Ulke

mother of Harriet Lane, were the first two children born of this marriage.

Harriet Lane, the youngest of four children, became an orphan in her tenth year. She attached herself voluntarily to her already distinguished uncle, who was at the time in the United States Senate, having but recently returned from Russia, where he had negotiated our first commercial treaty with that country.

Somewhat abashed though duly touched by the honor conferred upon him by his ardent little kinswoman, he undertook the novel responsibility of her upbringing with such misgivings as he had never been conscious of when accepting the various high honors bestowed upon him by his country. She quitted the home in Mercersburg, Pennsylvania, where she was born, and her uncle's home, Wheatland, became thenceforth hers. It was a roomy old brick house with ample grounds, on East King Street, in Lancaster, one of the old colonial towns of Pennsylvania.

It has been said, in no matter how many places we may live, there is only one that is home to us. Wheatland was that to Harriet Lane, though she was destined to see much of the world and to spend years at a time away from its tranquil seclusion. Its improvement and adornment were ever matters of keen interest to her. There she first attracted an admiration which gradually extended over her own country and England, for the fame of Harriet Lane was international. There she had possession of her uncle, it being their custom to spend their mornings together, usually in reading the newspapers, she incidentally absorbing his statesmanlike view of the political questions of the day.

Buchanan frequently entertained at Wheatland both his political friends and those he had made through his diplomatic relations. His niece was a truly betwitching hostess on these occasions, to which there often attached much that was brilliant.

The first attempt at training after she passed under her uncle's care was not a happy one in the estimation of his young ward. Being obliged to go to Washington for the session of Congress, he closed his home at Lancaster and transferred his *ménage* to the capital, for Buchanan always set up his household gods wherever he tarried for any length of time, his housekeeper, Miss Hetty Parker, who served him in that capacity for forty years, going with him from place to place. Harriet was left in Lancaster, in the home of some venerable spinsters of her uncle's acquaintance, who had pronounced ideas on the moral gait to be maintained by the rising generation. From her own accounts, given in letters to her uncle, she seems to have been frequently disciplined by means of her healthy young appetite. There were melodramatic occasions when she went without sugar in her tea, and was compelled to practise various similar mortifications of the flesh for which no small girl has a natural bent. After she was removed from these uncongenial surroundings she lived for some time in dread of an adverse circumstance that might return her to them. Her uncle, on whom neither the pathos nor the humor of the situation was lost, more than once suggested quizzically in his letters to her that she might like to go back to the old ladies.

When they were separated he wrote to her every day, at first from conscientious motives of the duty he owed to her, and later because of the pleasure he derived from this frequent interchange of thought and sympathy. When she was twelve years old he sent her with her sister, Mary, to boarding-school at Charlestown, West Virginia.

"Had Mary written to me that you were a good girl and had behaved yourself entirely well, I should have visited you during the Christmas holidays," he said, in the course of a letter written to her shortly after her initiation into boarding-school life.

In 1845 Buchanan became Secretary of State under President Polk. "My labors are great," he wrote to Harriet, shortly after entering upon the duties of his new office, "but they do not '*way*' me down, as you write the word. Now I would say ' *weigh*,' but doctors may differ on this point." Further on in the same letter he continues thus : " Your friends, Mrs. Bancroft [wife of the Secretary of War] and the Pleasantons often inquire for you. They have given you somewhat of a name here, and Mrs. Polk and Miss Rucker, her niece, have several times urged me to permit you to come and pass some time with them. I have been as deaf as the adder to their request, knowing, to use a word of your grandmother, that you are too ' outset-

ting' already. There is a time for all things under the
sun, as the wise man says, and your time will yet
come." Again, he sends love from Miss Hetty, his
housekeeper, and a message to the effect that she would
be glad to see Harriet in Washington. " I fear she
might be twice glad," added Buchanan, " once on
your arrival and still more so on your departure."

It was Buchanan's custom to spend his summers or a
portion of them at Bedford Springs, taking his nieces
with him. To the younger it has ever been a place of
happy memories. There, when she was still quite a
young girl, she met the man, then also full of all the
enthusiasm of youth, to whom, after exacting a prolonged devotion, she finally surrendered herself.

In one of her uncle's letters written to her in the
summer of 1846 he tells her he will not be able to go
to Bedford before the 10th of August, " when the season will be over and it will be too late for Mary to
enact the character of belle; and you," he continued,
" are quite too young to make the attempt."

He placed her, the autumn of that year, in the Visitation Convent, in Georgetown, whence she was graduated three years later with much distinction. She
passed one Sunday in every month during these three
years at her uncle's home on F Street, there catching
her first glimpse of that world of which she was later to
form a part. Her uncle was still Secretary of State, and
his home was frequented by the most illustrious men
who made up the public life of that day. There Harriet,
looking upon herself as a full-fledged young lady, spent

the first winter after her liberation from school duties. The following year, however, she passed quietly among her relatives in Pennsylvania, which was more in accord with her uncle's wishes, for she was still very young. The decision to do so was entirely voluntary on her part, which pleased Buchanan greatly, for he realized fully what a fascination the gay life of the capital held for a young girl in her high social position. He wrote her a letter full of praise for controlling what he knew to be her inclination and remaining at home. "This act of self-restraint has raised you in my estimation," he wrote, and then went on to relate frankly how gay the city was, and concluded by assuring her that Mr. John Sullivan, an Irish gentleman famous for his dinners, would be inconsolable when he learned that she was not to be there that winter.

It is supposed that no American woman ever had more offers of marriage than Harriet Lane, and it is evident, from a letter written her by her uncle about this time, that suitors had already begun to present themselves. "I wish now to give you a caution," he wrote: "never allow your affections to become interested, or engage yourself to any person, without my previous advice. You ought never to marry any person who is not able to afford you a decent and immediate support. In my experience I have witnessed the long years of patient misery and dependence which fine women have endured from rushing precipitately into matrimonial connections without sufficient reflection. Look ahead and consider the future, and act wisely in this particular."

With the incoming of Taylor's administration Buchanan retired to Wheatland, spending the ensuing four years there with occasional sallies to Washington and his summers as usual at Bedford Springs.

Harriet Lane was already a belle of far more than local repute when in 1852, her uncle having been appointed minister to England, she accompanied him thither.

Through the effect she produced in a strange land Buchanan probably for the first time fully realized how unusually beautiful she was. So favorable was the impression she made upon the queen that on state occasions she was assigned to places usually given only to the wives of ambassadors and ministers. She was well known throughout England, and on the day that Oxford University conferred the degree of Doctor of Civil Laws upon her uncle and Alfred Tennyson its ancient walls rang with the cheers that went up from its hundreds of students who rose *en masse* to greet the entrance of Harriet Lane.

"She was a most distinguished young person," said one of her countrymen recently, growing enthusiastic over the recollection of the impression she created, "whom more than one Englishman would have given his head to marry."

Her beauty was not less appreciated by the artistic eye of the French people, and Mr. James Edward MacFarland, who was secretary of the American legation at the time of her visit to the family of Mr. John Y. Mason, then our minister to France, was full of anecdotes of the *naïveté* with which the people in the streets of Paris were wont to express their admiration.

Shortly after her return to America the loss of her only sister, Mrs. George W. Baker, who died in California, sent Harriet Lane into deep mourning. While the country was filled with stories of her beauty and the impression it had created in foreign capitals she was passing her days in the grateful quiet of Wheatland. Her uncle's nomination to the Presidency but added to her fame, the campaign, election, and inauguration bringing her gradually into that eminent position she was so admirably fitted to fill. At the ball attending the inaugural ceremonies at Washington she made her first reappearance in public, clad, as best became her noble form, in the simplicity of a white dress, flower trimmed, and with a necklace of pearls.

In those days, before social functions had attained the proportions that now characterize them, they reflected in the White House, as elsewhere, more of the individuality of the host and hostess than is now possible. Many details that are now consigned to secretaries and stewards then appertained to the master and mistress of the house. Harriet Lane and her cousin James Buchanan Henry, who acted as private secretary to his uncle, invariably arranged the seating of the guests at state dinners, an onerous task now performed by an under-secretary of the Executive Mansion, who, besides being familiar with the rules of official precedence, must also know something of the social relationship each guest bears to his possible neighbor. She made no mistakes, for she had been trained to her position as had none of her predecessors, unless we except the wives of the two Adamses.

In 1860, when the Prince of Wales visited England's North American possessions, on President Buchanan's suggestion and invitation, he extended his travels so as to include at least a portion of the United States. The memory of his sojourn among us still lives in many of the cities and towns whose territory had once formed part of the kingdom of his ancestors. The five days he spent in Washington were passed in the White House. A guest of the nation at the capital is usually assigned to a suite of rooms in one of the hotels of the city. Between Buchanan and the Prince of Wales, however, owing to the former's recent residence at the court of St. James, there existed more of a personal feeling than is usual between the President and state guests.

In all the festivities by which the Executive Mansion did honor to his presence the unerring hand and faultless taste of Harriet Lane were evident.

One memorable day of his visit was spent at Mount Vernon. The revenue cutter "Harriet Lane" was selected to take the distinguished little party, consisting of the President, Miss Lane, the Prince, his suite, and the British Minister down the river. The simplicity of George Washington's home and the picturesque beauty of its situation were themes of interesting study to the Englishmen. At his tomb they reverently bared their heads, and near it the Prince planted a tree in remembrance of the day.

After he left Washington he wrote to the President expressing his appreciation of the hospitality he had received, and sending him his portrait painted by Sir John Watson Gordon, with a set of engravings of the Royal family for Miss Lane, to whom now also belong the portrait and the letter, together with one written by the queen. It echoes the gratification already expressed by her son concerning the kindliness of his reception among the American people, and shows in what high regard she personally held both the President and his niece.

Buchanan's administration was the last of the old *régime*, a period in which there had been that unity of purpose that had fostered the nation, that wise forebearance that had preserved it, and withal much of illustrious oratory and brilliant debate. But the parting of the ways had come. A day of action was at hand. Buchanan, oppressed with a sense of his impotency to avert a crisis that was inevitable, retired to Wheatland, and Lincoln, full of high purposes and many misgivings, stepped into the pathway of destiny. Upon the one public life instantly relaxed its hold, while about the other it threw its myriad feverish tendrils, clutching him hourly closer to itself till the long watches of that fatal April night, during which its imperious tenure was loosened by death.

With Buchanan, Harriet Lane also passed from the horizon of public life, spending with him at Wheatland those historic four years that followed her days in the White House. There, in January, 1866, she was married to Henry Elliott Johnston, of Baltimore. The ceremony was performed by her uncle, the Rev. Edward Y. Buchanan, of the Episcopal Church.

Her honeymoon she passed in Cuba and her married life in Baltimore, in whose social doings she took a prominent part. At her uncle's death, in 1868, she inherited Wheatland, where for a number of years she passed her summers. In 1892 she bought a home in Washington, where she now spends the greater part of her time.

Much has been given her of life's joys and triumphs, and much, too, of its sorrows. Death has repeatedly crossed the threshold of her home, robbing her, one by one, of her heart's treasures: in 1881 the elder of her two sons, James Buchanan Johnston, a boy of brilliant promise, then in his fourteenth year; in 1882 her second son, Henry Elliott Johnston; and two years later her husband. Surrounded not only by life's comforts, but its elegancies, by friends of her own and a succeeding generation, there is yet about Harriet Lane Johnston to-day much of that same majestic isolation that marked her youth.

ADÈLE CUTTS

(MRS. ROBERT WILLIAMS)

DURING the four years that Franklin Pierce presided over the nation so many beautiful women came prominently before the public at the capital that his was called the "beauty administration." Many were the wives and daughters of men in high official position, but the fame of none exceeded that of the daughter of James Madison Cutts, who held the office of Second Controller of the Treasury.

Born within a stone's throw of the White House, all her young days centred about it, and how near she came to living there as the wife of a President we may gauge by how near Stephen A. Douglas came to possessing that office. Adèle Cutts flourished in that truly golden era before material wealth became a necessary adjunct to a woman's popularity, when men were distinguished by a greater spirit of gallantry and disinterestedness, and in the days before a belle's powers at a watering-place were rated by the number or size of the trunks she took with her; in a word, in the days when the woman herself was pre-eminent and the accident of worldly possessions secondary.

It was recently said of a wealthy American girl, who, though she has generously expended much of her large fortune in the endowment of seats of learning and similar public benefactions, has yet in herself none of that magnetism that would entitle her to enrolment among the great belles of her country, " Yes, she is a great belle this summer. She brought thirty trunks, and she dresses six times a day." At the same resort forty years ago, Adèle Cutts, remarkable for the simplicity of her toilettes even among a generation that had no conception whatever of the elaborate costuming of women which marks the close of the century, was the most renowned of its belles.

While she derived in the preliminary stages of her social career some prestige from her connection with two of the most illustrious families not only of Virginia but of the entire country,—Washington and Madison,—she attained while yet a very young woman a pre-eminence by reason of her beauty, the distinction of her bearing, and a genuine loveliness of character, which reflected as much honor upon the somewhat remote relationship as it had bestowed upon her. She was born in the home of her grandfather, Richard Cutts, who, in the days when Maine was part of Massachusetts, had for twelve years represented in the Congress of the United States that district which at this end of the century was for so long a period associated with the name of Thomas B. Reed.

In 1804 Richard Cutts married Anna Payne, the youngest sister of the famous Dolly Payne, who some years before had become the wife of James Madison. Still another sister had married George Steptoe Washington, the nephew of our first President. It was of her sister Anna's family that Mistress Dolly wrote her lines adapted from John Gilpin's ride:

> " My sister Cutts and Cutts and I and Cutts's children three
> Will fill the coach, so you must ride on horseback after we."

The home Cutts built for his bride, and where his children and grandchildren were born, was in those early days one of the pretentious houses of the capital. It overlooked Lafayette Square, and its beautiful garden, where Addie Cutts played as a little girl, skirted along H street to the end of the block. Cutts was a widower when his son James Madison married Miss Ellen O'Neale, of Maryland, and took her to " Montpelier" to spend their honeymoon days with his aunt and uncle, whose namesake he was. On their return to Washington his bride became the mistress of her father-in-law's home, where in the following year, 1835, Adèle Cutts was born.

In the guise of a little flower-girl she made her first formal appearance at the White House when she was but seven years old, at a children's fancy ball given there in 1842 during the administration of President Tyler.

She was for the most part educated at Madame Burr's school, in the city in which she was born. Her wonderful grace of manner, however, was not the result of education; it was the manifestation of a character beautiful by nature and developed amid happy surroundings. An only daughter, she was the close companion of her beautiful and brilliant mother, besides spending much of her time until her fifteenth year with her great-aunt Madison, whose genius had sown the first seeds of social life in the barren wastes of the national capital and drawn together the scattered elements of its subsequent levees and dinner-parties. After the death of Madison, finding herself unable to support the solitude of her life at "Montpelier," which had been theretofore most complete and happy, she returned to Washington and took up her home in the Cutts house, which now belonged to her and which bears her name to this day, though it has had many other distinguished occupants. Richard Cutts had mortgaged it to Madison, and dying before he had repaid him, the house passed into the possession of Mrs. Madison. There she held a court as brilliant as any ever presided over by an American woman, and Adèle Cutts was early familiarized with the greatness of a generation that was already passing away. Webster, Clay, Calhoun, as well as every President of the United States whose term of office fell during her residence in Washington, paid her the tribute of frequent visits, and felt honored by his privilege to do so.

At the time of her death her great-niece was fourteen years old, and already possessed a beauty of the purest Greek type, whose stateliness increased as she advanced towards womanhood. The faultless outline of her profile, the shapeliness of her head, her large, dark eyes, her chestnut hair that showed glints of a golden hue in the sunshine, the creamy tone of her skin, the per-

Adèle Cutts
(Mrs. Robert Williams)
From portrait by George Peter A. Healy

fect proportion and development of her tall figure, all combined to make the rare beauty of a personality whose charm was augmented twofold by her own unconsciousness of its rich possessions.

Like many girls of southern proclivities, she spent her summers at that famous old resort that has witnessed the rising and going down of so many social stars, the White Sulphur Springs. There, dressed always in white, with a white kerchief in the mornings folded across her bosom and showing her fair throat, there was about her a freshness and simplicity that suggested her descent from the Quaker Paynes.

The spirit of gallantry has no age limit in the South, and she, like many another girl in the blossom of her youth, received the homage of men of all periods of life. The beautiful Imogene Penn, afterwards Mrs. James Lyons, of Richmond, and whose belleship days were contemporaneous with those of Adèle Cutts, encountered the irrepressible Richmond wag, Tom August, one morning as she was returning from the spring-house between two devotees, one of whom was the unsuspected possessor of forty-five, while the other concealed about his person as many as fifty summers. " I thought, Miss Imogene," said August, bowing profoundly to the trio and availing himself of a wit's privilege, " that you were just eighteen, but I see you are between forty-five and fifty."

Some Virginia beaux, who were young then, have treasured up and still relate an anecdote of the manner in which one of Adèle Cutts's elderly admirers lost the only opportunity she ever gave him to propose to her. He came from New Orleans, and was blessed with many good things, including sons and daughters older than Miss Cutts. At a fancy-dress ball she appeared completely disguised in the character of a housekeeper, having borrowed the entire costume, including the cap, apron, and bunch of keys at her side, from the housekeeper of the hotel. Before any one had had an opportunity to speculate on her identity, discovering her old admirer among the spectators of the gay and bewildering scene, she approached demurely and asked him if he did not need a housekeeper. He parried the question somewhat playfully, and ended by answering in the negative. She dropped him a courtesy with a grace no housekeeper could emulate, peeping at him with laughing eyes over her mask, and disappeared in the throng of the ball-room.

At a White House reception, early in the winter of 1856, she met Stephen A. Douglas, who was then prominent as a Presidential possibility; he was also one of the Illinois Senators, and his ringing speeches had won him a national fame equal to the intensity of his local popularity. His able defence of Andrew Jackson on the floor of the Senate so gratified and touched the old President that he preserved a copy of the speech, laying it aside as an inheritance for those who should come after him, and endorsing it as a defence of himself and his administration. The one great fault of that administration, in his own estimation, was none of those for which popular opinion of his day condemned him, but that he had not hanged Calhoun. "Douglas," writes one of his biographers, "had wonderfully magnetic powers, and usually carried his audience with him." It is small wonder, then, that at the end of a few months of ardent and eloquent debate, with an audience consisting of one young girl, that he should have carried her completely with him.

He was a widower with two sons when he met Adèle Cutts, and, like many a less fortunate man, he was instantly impressed with her absolute loveliness. He would go to her direct from the Senate chamber while the whole city was ringing with the fame of his speeches, which she not infrequently heard from a place in the gallery, and throw all his irresistible eloquence into his courtship of her.

In the Democratic Convention of the summer of 1856 Douglas and Buchanan were rival candidates for the Presidential nomination. Pierce, also, though there had been some doubt in the minds of his own townsmen about his making a successful President at all, was seeking the nomination for a second term. "Frank Pierce is all very well up here where he knows everybody and everybody knows Frank Pierce," said a New Hampshire sage during the summer preceding Pierce's election, "but when it comes to spreading him out over the whole country, I'm afraid he'll be mighty thin in some places." The thinness had evidently been apparent, for while he had the high honor of coming in almost unanimously, as Senator Benton said, he went out with as great a unanimity.

When it became evident that the nomination was not for Douglas, so intensely was he beloved by the people of the West, and particularly by those of his own State, that many a sturdy, hard-featured delegate from that section, to all appearances the embodiment of stoicism, put down his head and wept like a little heart-broken child.

On the 20th of November, a few weeks after the election of Buchanan, he was married to Adèle Cutts, and it has been said that, of the many beautiful women who witnessed the incoming of Buchanan's administration at his inaugural ball, Douglas's wife was the most beautiful.

Already known to the South and the East, her fame now spread westward, and when it was rumored that Douglas would take her to Chicago, where he had maintained a legal residence for some years, the people of the town made ready to receive her with the enthusiasm which she inspired in them then primarily as the young wife of Stephen A. Douglas. She made her first appearance among them at St. Mary's Church, where many people who had never been in a Catholic church before were found in the congregation that Sunday morning, and far more than the usual external contingent waited patiently on the sidewalk to see her as she came out. When she appeared with her husband at the celebration held on the State line between Illinois and Wisconsin, in honor of the union of the two railroad companies between Chicago and Milwaukee, she was hailed with uproarious cheers. There was that in her very presence which seemed to completely satisfy every man's ideal of all womanly perfection.

It was in the year of the great contest for the Legislature between Lincoln and Douglas that the people of the West came to know her, however, as she was already known at the East, and to love her with that same loyalty and devotion. Her home in Chicago was always in hotels, sometimes at the Tremont House and again at the Lake View. Many of the men who have made Chicago the queen city she is to-day were then young. Among them were professional men and men full of commercial enterprise, all brainy and ambitious, and a fair number of them Democrats and followers of Douglas. These gathered about her in her parlors or under the trees in the garden overlooking the lake, and though she never entered into any political discussion, the very fact that Douglas possessed such a wife inspired them with renewed ardor for his cause. In her gentle graciousness, infinite tact, and entire unconsciousness of the admiration she everywhere aroused, they felt the full force of her high breeding.

Lincoln and Douglas are so conspicuously identified as political enemies, that few people realize that personally they were friends. Not unfrequently they travelled a whole day together only to take the platform that night against each other and to pommel each other, figuratively, out of recognition. Douglas was adroit, however, and Lincoln once said of him that it was difficult to get the best of him in any debate, because his power of bewildering his audience was so great that they never knew when he was worsted. During the summer in which their political enmity first achieved so much prominence, Douglas's wife went with him through the State winning favor for him in all eyes, even including those of the " ablest whig rascal in all Springfield, Abe Lincoln." He liked to sit beside her as they journeyed from place to place and pour some funny story into her attentive ears, or, perhaps, divining the tender sympathy of her true woman's soul, tell her some incident of his early days, touching off its sorrowful details with a bit of homely philosophy or a stroke of his inexhaustible humor ; and as the train pulled into some expectant town, and the two opponents were greeted by factions whose enmity was real, he would say, " Here, Douglas, take your woman," and so they would part to meet again as foes. As the final victory was with Douglas, he and his wife made that tour of the Southern States that was much in the nature of a triumphal procession, and was a forerunner of his Presidential campaign which shortly followed.

His real home was in Washington, where as a Senator he spent the greater portion of each year. There he built a commodious house, with a ball-room, by no means a frequent adjunct at that time, which witnessed much generous hospitality in those difficult days preceding secession, when a woman like Mrs. Douglas could best hold warring elements in abeyance.

The result of the campaign of the summer of 1860, in which Lincoln and Douglas again confronted each other, this time for the higher prize of the Presidency, precipitated that crisis which at length brought these two life-long opponents together in defence of the Union. The whole aim of Douglas's life had been for the Presidency. He had accomplished all else he had ever set his heart upon, and he was so absolutely the idol of the people that it had not seemed possible to him he should fail here. He swallowed the bitterness of his disappointment heroically, however, and was a generous and even a graceful friend to Lincoln.

It is related that, when Lincoln rose to read his inaugural address, he hesitated a moment, uncertain as to what disposition to make of his hat; it was a new, high silk hat, too elegant an acquisition to the mind of one reared in the more than frugal atmosphere of Lincoln's home to be intrusted to the pine boards of the flag-draped stand in front of him. Douglas, divining the mental process of which Lincoln himself, in the embarrassment of the moment, was scarcely conscious, stepped forward and relieved him of the hat, holding it for him till the conclusion of the address.

During the early days of the conflict between the North and the South, which he had patriotically done his utmost to avert, he aided Lincoln with able counsel, pointing out to him among other things the necessity of securing Fortress Monroe and cautioning him against bringing the troops through Baltimore, prophesying that bloodshed that did occur. But before the conflict had assumed those proportions which it did later in the same year, on the 3d of June, 1861, Douglas's life closed.

His last hours were spent in Chicago among the people he had so ably represented. There, with his wife beside him, and her mother and brother, James Madison Cutts, who was his private secretary, near by, and with his keen, dark eyes upon her face, as if he would forever fix upon his spirit its beautiful lineaments, and his hand in hers, his mind retaining all its strength and clearness till the end, he uttered his last memorable words. She had asked him if he had any message to send to his sons, and he replied, " Tell them to obey the laws of the land and to support the Constitution of the United States."

Generous even to the point of recklessness, he died poor. Subscriptions were immediately begun among his friends towards a fund for his widow. She declined, however, to receive it, and begged that the sum thus raised be devoted to the erection of a monument to Douglas's memory.

She returned to Washington and lived quietly for some years in the first home of her married life, taking no part in the social world whose magnet she had been for so many seasons. But she was not forgotten; and when she again, after four years of seclusion, resumed her place in its midst, her reappearance brought up innumerable memories of her earlier days, of her conquest of the " Little Giant," and of her queenly part in his political campaigns.

She was the guest of honor at a dinner given in the early winter of 1865, just as the war drew to its close, by Miss Harris, whose name lives in history in a very different connection: she was sitting beside Lincoln in his box at the theatre on the night he was shot. Among the guests bidden to meet Mrs. Douglas was Captain, afterwards General, Robert Williams, one of the handsomest and most gallant officers of the army, and a member of a well-established family of Culpeper County, Virginia. Mrs. Douglas was already known to him by fame, and suspecting her to be possessed of all the caprices of a spoiled beauty, he had no desire whatever to meet her, though he accepted Miss Harris's invitation for the sake of the pleasure he would otherwise derive from her hospitality. After he had been presented to Mrs. Douglas, however, whatever enjoyment he had anticipated from meeting others there passed from his mind. Combined with a gentle dignity, there was about her all the sweet simplicity of a young girl, and nothing that ever so remotely suggested any consciousness of a fame that was as wide as her country. He followed her with all the earnestness with which he had meant to avoid her, and in January, 1866, she again became a bride.

The chronicle of the most magnificent ball ever given, not only in Washington, but probably in the country, and which occurred shortly after her marriage to General Williams, hands her name and that of Kate Chase Sprague down to fame as the two most beautiful women who participated in the brilliant event. It was given by the French minister, Count de Moutholon, by order of his Emperor, in honor of the officers of the French fleet then anchored at Annapolis.

She gradually, however, abdicated her social queenship for a crown she wore with no less grace, that of a
most noble motherhood.

Wedded to an army man, her life led her from post to
post, and the greater part of her days from that time
was spent in the West.

The little life of the only child of her first marriage
covered but a few months. The six children of her
second marriage, however, are all living and grown to
manhood and womanhood, two of her sons being in
the military service of their country.

The last few years of her life were passed in Washington, where her husband held the office of Ad-
jutant-General until his retirement from the service.
There her eldest daughter was married, in January, 1899,
to Lieutenant John Bryson Patton, and there also, on
the 26th of the same month, her own life terminated.
Time had touched her lightly, as if he would not rob
her of a loveliness that had been as much a charm to
women as to men. Asked once the secret of her
youthful appearance, she blushed like a girl and confessed that she was happy, and that therein must lie the
solution.

It is difficult to analyze the qualities of that power
of fascination which some women have exercised over
the world. They are as varied as the individuality of
the women to whom they have been intrusted. In
Adèle Cutts, however, they seem to have emanated
from a singular beauty of soul, a species of primal in-
nocence that proclaimed itself at once to the sense of

every beholder and preserved her alike from any touch of vanity or worldliness.

To those who knew her she seemed little changed as the years rolled on, because to her classic beauty of form was added an indestructible quality which was a beauty of the spirit.

EMILIE SCHAUMBURG

(MRS. HUGHES-HALLETT)

EVERY Philadelphia girl who has hoped to be a belle during this last quarter of the century, and even many who have been without social aspirations, have been brought up on traditions of Emilie Schaumburg.

Yet so eminent was the place she held in the old city whose standard of belleship had been fixed far back in the colonial days of America, that no one has ever succeeded her.

Accustomed through long generations to women of wit, beauty, and a certain unapproachable taste in matters of personal adornment, Philadelphia has developed a critical instinct which is not easily satisfied

"The ladies of Philadelphia," wrote Miss Rebecca Franks over a century ago, "have more cleverness in the turn of an eye than those of New York have in their whole composition. With what ease have I seen a Chew, a Penn, an Oswald, or an Allen, and a thousand others, entertain a large circle of both sexes; the conversation, without the aid of cards, never flagging nor seeming in the least strained or stupid. Here, in New York, you enter the room with a formal set courtesy, and, after the how-dos, things are finished; all is dead calm till the cards are introduced, when you see pleasure dancing in the eyes of all the matrons, and they seem to gain new life."

It is but just to state that this fair critic of New York's social status belonged to Philadelphia, where, though her wit was rather of a satirical turn, she was noted as a lady possessed of " every human and divine advantage." She was the youngest of the three daughters of David Franks, one of whom became the wife of Oliver de Lancey, another of Andrew Hamilton, of " Woodlands," one of the famous suburban estates of the city, while Rebecca, "high in toryism and eccentricity," after an unusually brilliant belleship, bestowed her hand on Lieutenant-General Sir Henry Johnston, and went to live in England.

Of the Chews referred to in her letter from New York, so sparkling was the conversation which Harriet could maintain, that Washington, when he was sitting for his portrait to Stuart, liked to have her in the room that his face might wear its most agreeable expression, such as her wit always induced. She married the son of Charles Carroll of Carrollton, the young Charles Carroll who was at one time suspected of having a tender interest in Nellie Custis, Washington's stepgranddaughter. Her sister Margaret, who was one of the beauties who made the great feast of the Mischianza so famous, also married a son of Maryland, Colonel John Eager Howard, a patriot and a hero. Passing through her room one evening he heard her relating to her children the pathetic story of Major André, who had been her knight in the tournament of the Mischianza.

"Don't believe a word of it, children," he interrupted, as their young hearts swelled with pity at her graphic and romantic recital ; " he was an infernal spy."

Ann Willing, who married William Bingham in her seventeenth year, was another woman who helped to establish the standard of female beauty and excellence in Philadelphia. "She is coming quite into fashion here," John Adams's daughter wrote of her from London, "and is very much admired. The hair-dresser who dresses us on court days inquired of mamma whether she knew the lady so much talked of here from America, Mrs. Bingham. He had heard of her from a lady who had seen her at Lord Duncan's."

London society, and especially that of the court circle, was not very favorably disposed towards Americans in the year 1786, and the subsequent graciousness of their reception they doubtless owed largely to the impression created by the beauty and character of such a woman as Mrs. Bingham, who was one of the first to seek a presentation at the court of George III. after our separation from the mother-country. Her striking beauty of face and form, her easy deportment, that had all the pride and grace of high breeding, the intelligence of her countenance, and the entire affability of her attitude disarmed every feeling of unfriendliness and converted every one, said Mrs. Adams, into admiration.

The unfortunate Margaret Shippen, as gifted as she was beautiful, deprived by her husband's treason before she was twenty years old of the shelter of her home and the protection of her family, the Executive Council of Pennsylvania bidding her to leave the State and not return till the close of the war, and Sarah, the daughter of Benjamin Franklin and wife of Richard Bache, and the embodiment of Republican principles, which caused her to insist that there was " no rank in America but rank mutton," are two noted examples of that diversity which gave flavor to the social life of a city that has tempted the pens of both native and foreign critics.

Philadelphia was one of the first of the Northern cities to admit women to the pit of its theatres, and visitors from quiet Boston and commercial New York at one time condemned its social tone as fast, because its young men gave wine-suppers, and because it danced to the music of a full colored orchestra, known as Johnson's Band, while other cities were performing their more or less graceful gyrations to the tunes furnished by one or two musicians."

The Quaker town had made a brilliant social record before many of the cities of America had so much as laid one stone upon another. By comparison it is old. It has its elements of newness, like all bodies that grow and progress, but they are not readily assimilated by that little coterie that long ago laid the foundation of its establishment in the southeastern section of the city. It is from the predominance of this conservative social principle in Philadelphia that people unfamiliar with its life have derived the erroneous impression that its general progress and development have been correspondingly deliberate.

To hold such a position as Emilie Schaumburg held in Philadelphia implies the possession of such personal qualities and such gifts as would be an open door to the most exclusive society of the world.

She was well born, coming of ancestry distinguished both in their native land and in that of their adoption. Her grandfather, Colonel Bartholomew Schaumburg, belonged to one of the oldest families in Germany. He was a godson and ward of the Landgrave Frederick William, with whom he was closely connected. When still quite a youth, the Landgrave made him an aide-de-camp to Count Donop, who commanded the Hessian subsidies furnished by Germany to England to aid her in the war with the American colonies.

Schaumburg was sent with despatches to Donop, who, however, had been killed before the arrival of his young aide-de-camp. Learning for the first time of the righteousness of the American cause, he gallantly offered his services to the commander-in-chief of the American forces. He fought valiantly all through the war, and at its close accepted a commission in the standing army organized by the new government. At the Cotton Centennial held at New Orleans in 1884, his commissions signed by Washington were exhibited and were objects of much interest. He took part in many of the early Indian wars, and was appointed quartermaster-general in the war of 1812.

His home was at New Orleans. His eldest daughter,

Emilie Schaumburg
(Mrs. Hughes-Hallett)
From portrait by Waugh

at the time of General Lafayette's visit to that city, was one of the twelve young girls selected on account of their beauty from its most distinguished families to crown America's friend. She lived to an advanced age, surviving her eleven companions of that memorable occasion and retaining much of her beauty till the close of her life.

The site of the city of Cincinnati was indirectly chosen by Colonel Schaumburg when he selected the spot where it later sprung up for the establishment of a fort, which he called, in honor of his first American friend, Fort Washington.

He was an accomplished artillerist, and under his direction was cast the first cannon made in the United States. While stationed in Carlisle, Pennsylvania, upon military duty, he met the lady whom he afterwards married, and who had not long previously arrived in America, whither she had come with her parents to trace a recent acquisition of land.

She was a lineal descendant of the principal Indian chief, Secaneh, of the Lenape tribe, who signed the treaty of 1683 with William Penn, selling him the large tract of land on which Philadelphia is built.

The Princess Susahena, the daughter of Secaneh, had been married to Thomas Holme McFarlane, a nephew of Thomas Holme, who was the first Surveyor-General of Pennsylvania. Three years after their marriage they sailed for Dublin, but ocean voyages in those days were trials to the stoutest constitutions, and the poor princess died before reaching the other side.

Her child, a daughter, lived, and it was the great-granddaughter of this child who became the wife of Colonel Schaumburg, so that Emilie Schaumburg is the seventh generation in lineal descent from the aboriginal princess, and attained her remarkable social queenship on the native heath of her royal ancestors.

Mrs. Henry D. Gilpin, who had known Colonel Schaumburg's family intimately and had spent much time with them in their Southern home, frequently spoke of the great beauty of Emilie Schaumburg's grandmother, and of the resemblance Emilie bore to her. She had the fresh Irish complexion and violet eyes, together with suggestions of the Indian type of her ancestry in the tall, lithe figure, delicately aquiline features, and black hair, which almost swept the ground.

They were a strikingly handsome couple, for Colonel Schaumburg was as magnificent in appearance as he was conspicuous in courage. He was several inches over six feet in height, and clung all his life to powdered hair and lace ruffles, those outward signs of the aristocrat; yet he adopted republican principles, dropped his title, and besought his children to be satisfied with the record he should leave them of services rendered his adopted country.

He had declined the overtures made him by his family in Germany, from whom he had become estranged owing to the course he had pursued in espousing the American cause. He had no desire to return and resume his career there.

When his granddaughter, however, visited Germany

she was received with marked consideration by the Princess of Schaumburg-Lippe, who was reigning at the time.

True to his principles, Colonel Schaumburg opposed the formation of the Society of the Cincinnati, refusing to become a member of it, and arguing that it had for its object the inauguration of an aristocracy, and was in direct opposition to the very principles for which they had fought.

His son followed in his footsteps in selecting a military career. He was graduated from the National Military Academy in 1833, and entered the cavalry. He was a gallant officer, generous and impetuous, and as magnificent in physique as his father.

He lost his commission through a technicality which the War Department turned to his disadvantage, and fought all his life for reinstatement, being upheld by President Jackson and a majority of the United States Senate.

He had imbibed his father's ideas, and would never use the "von" in his name because his father had dropped it. When his daughter wished to resume it, however, he gave his consent and approval.

Major Schaumburg married a daughter of Stephen Page, originally of Page County, Virginia, and later of Eden Park, a beautiful country-seat, near Philadelphia, where his children were born. Miss Page, who became Mrs. Schaumburg, was a woman of much beauty and many accomplishments, which she transmitted to her daughter.

Emilie von Schaumburg grew up in the home of her

uncle, Colonel James Page, with whom her name is ever identified. Though he was a man of social and political prominence, his greatest distinction, in the eyes of his fellow-citizens, arose from his relationship to her.

When this new fame dawned upon him, he had been for nearly fifty years a well-known and popular figure in the life of the city. His military record had been made in his youth during the war of 1812. He had been Postmaster and Collector of the Port of Philadelphia, a leader in Councils, County Treasurer in an era when politics had gone hand in hand with principle and patriotism. He was a Jacksonian Democrat, and had come to be looked upon as the grand old man of his party, who by birth and breeding could adorn a ball at Madam Rush's or make an after-dinner speech with as ready a grace as he could march at the head of the State Fencibles.

In no capacity, however, did he attract that peculiar interest that pursued him whenever he appeared in public with his niece. On winter afternoons, at a time when that season was rather longer in the Middle States than it is at the close of the century, and when the waters of the rivers used to remain fast frozen for many days they frequently appeared among the skaters, of whom, in his youth, Colonel Page had been one of the celebrities. He found new enthusiasm in the graceful sport, however, from the admiration he read in all faces whenever he went upon the ice with his niece.

They formed a picture that many paused to look upon, while others, who knew nothing of the intricacies of the accomplishment, gathered on the river-bank solely for the pleasure of watching them as they took those wonderfully long, sweeping curves of the "outer edge," the lithe figure of the girl seeming to float like a bird on the wing, while the splendid poise of the handsome, vigorous old man was as erect, as easy, and as firm as in his youth. He always held that the highest art in skating was in perfecting, to an almost incredible degree, the delicate balance of the body on the outer edge of the skate, and so broadening and lengthening the curves, which are ever, according to Hogarth, the lines of beauty. The result justified the theory, and he found an apt pupil in his niece, whose skating, like her dancing, was the very poetry of motion.

The beauty of some women admits of a diversity of opinion. Emilie von Schaumburg's did not. It was absolute, and the effect was instantaneous. A head of classic mould, with its rich adornment of lustrous black hair, proudly poised upon a throat and shoulders of perfect form; an oval face, lighted with a fine vivacity and captivating smile; great hazel eyes with dark brows and sweeping lashes; delicate, regular features, and a complexion which no art could imitate in its transparent fairness and brilliancy; a figure, tall and svelt, all undulating lines and willowy grace; a regal carriage, and, above all, an air of high-bred elegance and distinction; such, in her early girlhood, was Emilie von Schaumburg, whom the Prince of Wales declared the most beautiful woman he had seen in America.

It was on that famous night when the visit of His Royal Highness to the Academy of Music brought thither one of the most distinguished audiences ever assembled in Philadelphia. She was dressed with girlish simplicity in white, her only ornament being a small chain of golden sequins, which bound the rich masses of her hair and defined her shapely head, yet such was the subtle power of her presence, that from the moment she entered that crowded assembly, with its tier upon tier of brilliantly arrayed women, she became the focus of all eyes, dividing the attention of the Prince of Wales and the audience with Patti, who was pouring out her soul in matchless melody upon the stage.

One night, a few years ago, during a performance of Madame Bernhardt, in Philadelphia, a woman occupying one of the boxes, and carrying herself with that fine spirit that had been the glory of a previous generation, was recognized as Emilie Schaumburg, for so she still is, and forever will be known, among the people of her own city and country.

The discovery flew from mouth to mouth, and many who had never before seen her, as well as those who looked upon her for the first time after many years, and recalled that memorable night at the Academy of Music, bent upon her a gaze of unmistakable admiration.

Her education was principally directed by Hon. Henry Gilpin, who was the Attorney-General of Van Buren's administration, and a most finished scholar.

To the many advantages she enjoyed in having access to his library she subsequently added a thorough knowledge of several modern languages, for her intellectual endowments were in no degree inferior to her physical gifts. Though she had a fine artistic sense and an almost incredible facility in the acquirement of knowledge, she yet early recognized the necessity of serious study and intelligent application.

In this recognition and the ability to comply with its requirements, perhaps, more than in any other thing, lies the vast difference between the mere butterfly of society and the woman who leaves the impress of her individuality upon the life in which she moves.

Emilie Schaumburg never attempted a thing for which she had no special talent, but, having once undertaken a study, she pursued it with enthusiasm, following its every detail to the limit of her capacity. To an admirer, who once exclaimed, " Is there anything in the world you cannot do, and do brilliantly?" she replied, " Yes: I was a dismal failure at both sewing and arithmetic."

Her voice, in speaking as in singing, lent itself to every delicate inflection. She would delight, when still a very young child, to imitate. Each new song she caught with an unerring ear, the florid passages, roulades, and trills flowing as easily and naturally from the childish throat as from that of a bird. This marvellously flexible quality of voice she has never lost. In speaking of her musical education, she once said to a friend,—

" I have had to study phrasing and style and expression, with sostenuto, crescendo, diminuendo, and various other artistic effects, but the drudgery of exercises was spared me, thanks to my fairy godmother."

She has always retained her habits of study, and even during her first brilliant season in Paris she found time to take lessons from Madame La Grange and also from the celebrated teacher Delle Sédié. Later, however, at Nice, she studied more consecutively with Maestro Gelli, who recognized the unusual order of her talents and wrote several beautiful *morceaux* expressly for her.

Her beauty and accomplishments were the open sesame to the exclusive circles of the villa society at Nice, and among the many distinguished people whom she delighted with her rare gifts was the late lamented Duke of Albany. Like most of the royal family of England, he was an accomplished critic and an ardent lover of music. He was enthusiastic in his praise of Miss von Schaumburg's singing, and when she again met him, a year or two later, at a court-ball at Buckingham Palace, his greeting proved that he had not forgotten the impression it had made upon him. His first words were, " And how is the beautiful voice ?"

Before she left Philadelphia her histrionic talents had perhaps made her more widely known than any other of her many accomplishments. During the war for the Union, when the stage was the means of raising many dollars for the benefit of the wounded and suffering soldiers, she was foremost among the bright and spirited society women who devoted their talents to the cause.

EMILIE SCHAUMBURG

Her dramatic success was due neither to her beauty nor to her personal charm, though her expressive features, her voice, and her perfect grace and ease were undoubtedly powerful adjuncts. Her triumphs were legitimate, and were the result of careful study, artistic finish, and unusual histrionic ability. That she possessed, in an extraordinary degree, the power of getting out of herself and into her parts was evidenced by the tribute contained in the criticism of some friends who went to see her in "Masks and Faces." They had gone, they said, solely to see Miss Schaumburg, whom, however, they soon forgot, their interest becoming absorbed in the brilliant, fascinating, impulsive Peg.

Yet Emilie Schaumburg was a very young girl when she stepped upon the amateur stage of the Seventeenth-Street Drawing-Room, and had never had a lesson in declamation nor a suggestion from any one to help her in the study of her parts. To be able to forget one's identity, and to make one's audience forget it, is, after all, the acme of high art in acting, or, rather, it is the touch of genius which is above art, since it can not be taught.

As Peg Woffington in "Masks and Faces," and as the Countess in the "Ladies' Battle," she carried conservative and critical audiences by storm. Ristori, who was present at one of the performances, expressed unqualified admiration at the high order of Miss Schaumburg's talent, for both *rôles* are considered tests to trained actresses.

She scored another success in the little operetta,

"Les Noces de Jeannette," which she sang and acted in French, and in which the *pièce de résistance* is the great *air du rossignol.* There are many people in Philadelphia to-day who yet recall the brilliancy and daring of those *tours de forces* between the voice and the flute, each one in turn taking up the refrain and soaring higher and higher in imitation of the nightingale; yet there was never a harsh or strained note in her perfect voice, but all as liquid, pure, and full-throated as the warbling of the veritable bird.

Another of the gifts she possessed was for versification. She brought it into frequent and graceful play, but only for the enjoyment of those who were admitted to the privilege of an intimate friendship with her.

It is little wonder that Emilie von Schaumburg should have made an impress upon the city of her nativity which has remained proof against time and absence. No woman ever won a more spontaneous admiration than fell to her lot. She never appeared upon the streets that she was not surrounded and followed by both men and women, who, frequently without knowing her, came simply to look upon her beauty and glory in her possession.

She married, in England, Colonel Hughes-Hallett, of the Royal Artillery, and member of Parliament for Rochester. She resides now during the greater part of the year at Dinard, in France, where she built, some years ago, the beautiful château of Montplaisir.

Still a strikingly handsome and distinguished woman, she gathers about her the aristocracy of both France and England as well as the most eminent and charming of her compatriots. She entertains during each season with that same graciousness of hospitality with which she once presided in her uncle's home in Philadelphia.

She recently added a ball-room to Monplaisir which she inaugurated by a series of concerts and balls, among the picturesque features of the latter being minuets, gavottes, and a cotillon.

Gowned in a white and silver brocade Watteau, with panniers, over a pink satin petticoat trimmed with flounces of old lace, headed with wreaths of roses of a deeper pink, her powdered hair crowned with a black Gainsborough hat with black, white, and pink plumes, Mrs. Hughes-Hallett took part in one of the stately gavottes, making a beautiful picture against the delicate blue background and Louis Quinze decorations of her artistic ball-room.

A life filled with adulation, that would have been the undoing of a less wise woman, has in no way impaired her charm of character. Her fine mental poise, her exquisite humor, together with the generosity and sweetness of her nature, have preserved her from that calamitous sense of satiety that has overtaken many a man and many a woman who have lost their balance completely in an altitude of admiration much below that in which Emilie von Schaumburg has passed her life.

KATE CHASE

(MRS. WILLIAM SPRAGUE)

THERE was a name in America a little more than a generation ago that possessed a power amounting almost to enchantment, the name of Kate Chase, a woman who holds a unique place in both the political and social history of this century. The story of her life, between the high lights of its early days and the shadows in which it closed, presents a peculiar succession of superlatives. There stands forth, however, through all its changes, one unvarying dominant feature which must strike us at once, whether we approach it in the spirit of a student or actuated merely by a passing curiosity: her absolute devotion to her father. Through our knowledge of him, therefore, we may, in a measure, penetrate those mists in which she is enveloped by the divided opinion of a public, some of whom loved and idealized her as a social divinity, while others hated and maligned her as an opposing political force. Thus may we reach some just valuation of a character that with its man's virility and woman's delicacy was in itself singularly enigmatical, of its incentives and ideals, and, indirectly, therefore, of the failure and disappointments which have left their indelible stamp upon the life of Kate Chase.

In her father, profoundly cultured and endowed with

inexhaustible intellectual resources, she found the complete realization of her most exalted conception. She well knew the tenderness of the heart, the sensitiveness of the nature, he carried beneath that superb exterior of majestic and unapproachable dignity. She lived in close communion with the man, the angry rebuke of whose eye, says one of his biographers, no transgressor could support. She was the central feature of his remarkable home. Upon both of his daughters he expended a tenderness of devotion of which those who lived beyond the sphere of a personal acquaintance with him had no conception. Yet there have been inconspicuous women whom he might have fathered with more ultimate happiness to themselves than the remarkable daughter who is the subject of this sketch. Though he was a great man, winning justifiable distinction in every branch of the government of his country, he was yet not competent to cope with the problems which the life of such a woman as Kate Chase was continually presenting. In her presence alone, in the proud carriage of her regal head, there was that singular power that, while it drew forth the love and admiration that are the expression of a generous nature, likewise provoked in those of a baser order a hideous envy and hatred that assailed her even as a young girl. With his benignant belief in the universal goodness of mankind, Chase was singularly deficient in that knowledge of human nature which should have enabled him to throw about her that sort of aggressive protection which she peculiarly required.

There is one little incident in his life that throws light upon his own character, and upon the principle he pursued in directing his daughter. He was a man of the most delicate tastes and with a high appreciation of all the niceties of life. When he took the platform as an abolitionist, he was rotten-egged. Removing as much as possible of the offensive effusion with his handkerchief, he continued with what he was saying. He made no modification in his statements, nor did he close the window through which the unsavory missiles had made their entrance. As far as possible he ignored the occurrence.

The scandal-monger he treated with the same silent scorn, continuing the tenor of his life as if he had not been made aware of his existence. But while he, a courageous man, might walk fearlessly amid the storm of the angry nation that impeached Andrew Johnson, and, regardless of its threats, discharge the duties of his high office with that calmness that distinguished all the acts of his judicial career and adds to the glory of his name in the eyes of a later generation, his daughter, though no less courageous, was yet " too slight a thing" to defy the gossips of even one Western town. " Ah! little woman," she once said, laying her hand on the shoulder of one of her loyal friends to whom sorrow had come, " you, at least, have never made the mistake that I made. I never cared for the opinion or good-will of people. I ran my head against a stone wall. It did not hurt the wall but it has hurt the head." This is perhaps the nearest approach to self-justification she

ever made for having essayed, with a man's independence, to live that most circumscribed life of a conspicuously beautiful woman.

Losing her own mother when she was scarcely beyond
her infancy, and her step-mother before she had reached
womanhood, and realizing early that she was treated in
all things as his equal in years and understanding by the
man whose superiority among his fellow-men she conceived to be beyond question, that spirit of self-reliance
that is the natural outcome of all positive characters
was intensified in her to an abnormal degree. While it
gave her the fundamental qualifications of that leadership which she maintained with unparalleled brilliancy,
it likewise, through lack of direction, developed that
imperious tendency that proved so fatal to her own
happiness.

She was the first child of Chase's marriage to his
second wife, Eliza Ann Smith, and was named by her
mother after his first wife, Katherine Garniss, for whom
she had had a tender friendship and sincere admiration.

Of her birth, which occurred on the 13th of August,
1840, her father's journal contains the following record,
a characteristic statement of the event from a God-fear-
ing man whose knowledge, not only of children, but
of the human family in general, was largely drawn
from "judicious treatises."

"I went apart, and kneeling down prayed God to
support and comfort my dear wife, to preserve the life
of the child, and save both from sin. I endeavored to
give up the child and all into His hands. After a while

I went into the room. The birth had taken place at 2 A.M. on the 13th. After I had seen my wife and child, I went into the library and read a few pages in Eber's book on children, a judicious treatise. At last I became tired, and, though it was now day, lay down and slept awhile. The babe is pronounced pretty. I think it quite otherwise. It is, however, well formed, and I am thankful. May God give the child a good understanding that she may know and keep his commandments."

Of the early age at which Chase elected to test that understanding, his journal also furnishes an evidence. An entry therein, under date of November 24, 1845, about two months after her mother's death, shows the dawn of that remarkable intellectual intercourse which he maintained with his daughter till the end of his life. " This day," it reads, " has been marked by no extraordinary event. Rose, as usual of late, before sunrise; breakfasted with sister Alice and little Kate. Read Scriptures (Job) to little Kate, who listened and seemed to be pleased, probably with the solemn rhythm, for she certainly can understand very little; then prayed with her; then to town in omnibus, unshaven for want of time."

Within that same year he also recorded in his journal that he was teaching " dear little Kate to read verses in the Bible and listening to her recite poems."

Thus early, without any particular system probably, but wholly delightfully and under a most patient and winning master, begun the training of one of the most astute and brilliant minds with which a woman was

ever gifted. She was keen and clever rather than profound, and her quick intelligence caught and assimilated
the fruit of her father's years of study. Without having
his absorbing love of books, she yet read much and
forgot nothing. Chase used to say that in the miscel-
laneous reading of his boyhood, it was the pleasure he
derived from a stray law-book that determined his
choice of career. He pursued his profession with the
ardor of real love, and his daughter imbibed from him a
substantial knowledge of its technicalities. He used to
go over his cases with her very much at first in the
spirit in which he had read Job to her, later because he
delighted in her understanding, and finally because she
had become genuinely helpful to him.

Well ordered and simple was the atmosphere of the
home in which she grew up. As was his custom from
the time he established his own home till the end of his
life, Chase called his household together at the beginning of every day to ask the blessing and protection of
God. There were times, as seen from his journal, when
little Kate seems to have been his only companion, yet
the duty was never omitted.

She walked with him often to his office or to court in
the morning, both in Ohio and after they had removed
to Washington, talking sometimes of the things which
interested her, but more frequently of those which en-
grossed him, for it was his life and his ambitions that
gave color to both of their existences. He had taught
her early his favorite games, chess and backgammon,
which she often played with him in the quiet evenings

they spent together, or, if it were out of doors, croquet or some simple childish game, for she was part of the relaxation of his lighter hours as she was the repository of all the confidences and hopes of his public career.

His third marriage, in 1846, to Sarah Ludlow identified him with one of the prominent families of Cincinnati; Israel Ludlow, his wife's grandfather, having been one of the founders of the city. Chase, himself, though an Eastern man, born in Cornish, New Hampshire, whence he had migrated on coming of age, was now one of the prominent figures of Cincinnati, a busy, prosperous lawyer, with excellent political prospects, which met their first realization when, in 1849, he was elected to the United States Senate. When he came, six years later, into the governorship of his State he was again a widower, and Kate, though less than fifteen years of age, took her place at the head of his home.

Accustomed since the dawn of memory to the most considerate attentions from the most kingly of men, she already carried herself with that noble grace that made her presence felt in every assemblage above that of all others, no matter how simply she clothed herself nor how quietly she deported herself.

Chase was the first of Ohio's governors to take up his official residence at Columbus. There, for a year, Kate went as a day pupil to Mr. Heyl's seminary, and later studied in the same institution music and languages, having for the latter an unusual gift. She spoke French faultlessly, especially after her long residence abroad, which came later in her life. Her German, while

Kate Chase
(Mrs. William Sprague)
From photograph by Julius Ulke

it was fluent, had always a suggestion of a foreign accent that in her seemed rather pleasing than otherwise. Her native tongue she wielded with rare perfection, and no one who has heard Kate Chase talk will ever forget the magic of her voice, the life her graphic and discriminating language breathed into every thought to which she gave utterance, while her wonderful eyes expressed, even betrayed, every emotion. An old man who served the Chase family for years in the capacity of coachman once paid a tribute to the delicacy and power of her verbal delineations which many a man of more enlightened intelligence more gracefully, perhaps, but not more aptly acknowledged. He said he knew no greater pleasure than to take Miss Kate off in the carriage with a book in her lap, and, without opening it, for her to tell him every word that it contained from beginning to end.

The positive element of her character had already manifested itself by the time she was sixteen years old. She was, at about that period, out of compliment to her father, elected to the secretaryship of a charitable organization of women, all of whom were many years her senior. During the course of one of the meetings, a physician, of whose services the body had availed itself, and who had given offence to some of its members, was made the object of an abuse as senseless as it was verbose. The spirit of opposition was more timorous in the feminine organization of that day than it is in those that have been the outgrowths of later years, and Kate Chase, alone, had the courage to rise in defence of the absent doctor. Appealing to the chair to silence the undignified outburst, she won on the spot an ill-will that followed her long after those who cherished it had forgotten its original cause. But her young life was full of a sweet homage, and such a graceful tribute as was conveyed in the knowledge that one of the ex-governors of the State had named the most beautiful rose in his famous garden after her, easily atoned for the ill-will of a few people which seemed, after all, but a ripple on the ever-broadening surface of her life.

The growing strength of the Republican party, which had been ushered into existence in her father's law offices in Cincinnati, under the inspiration of Dr. Gamaliel Baily, revealed possibilities to a man of Chase's ambition and ability that haunted him thenceforth till the end of his life. Kate knew intimately the strong men who formed the nucleus of that great party. She knew its aims and purposes, and was in possession of its secret history contained in her father's letters and journals and in her own memory of its inception and progress. Yet nothing ever wrung them from her, though she was frequently approached by magazine editors with offers that would have been a temptation even to those in less need.

Her father's ambition became the absorbing object of her life, developing in her, before she had reached her twentieth year, a scientific knowledge of politics that no woman, and few men, have ever surpassed. " I know your bright mind," once wrote Roscoe Conkling, in submitting to her a political problem, "will solve this quicker than mine." It has been said that many details of the campaign of 1884, against Blaine, who was Conkling's political enemy, were planned at Edgewood.

To an intellect naturally endowed with many masculine qualities, she added a woman's quicker wit and greater powers of divination and an overmastering love for the father in whose interest she exercised every faculty of her gifted mind.

When the first convention of the Republican party met at Chicago, in 1860, to nominate a president, Chase was a prominent candidate for that honor. His daughter accompanied him to Chicago, and thence for the first time her name went forth over the land. His confidence in her, his reliance upon her, treating her in all respects more as if she were a son than a daughter, her youth, and the purely feminine quality of her beauty rendered her unique and conspicuous.

The choice of the new party fell upon Abraham Lincoln, and Seward, who supported him and opposed Chase's pretensions, received later the recognition of his services when he was tendered the first place in Lincoln's cabinet. Chase was, however, elected for the second time to the United States Senate, where he took his seat March 4, 1861. Two days later he had resigned and gone into Lincoln's cabinet as Secretary of the Treasury. His home was thus transferred to Washington, where, going later on the Supreme Bench, he passed the balance of his days, neither he nor his children ever returning to

Ohio. Chase was even laid to rest in Washington, and slept over thirteen years in beautiful Oak Hill. In the fall of 1886, however, his daughter had him removed to Ohio, that he might rest finally in the State that had been his home and that was associated with his early fame. There, a few months ago, she was laid by his side.

At the capital of the nation Kate Chase attained a social prestige never before enjoyed by so young a woman, and a political power which no woman before or since her day has ever possessed. Men of such eminence and distinction paid her the court of an homage so absolute that it would be difficult to estimate how much of her father's prominence was owing to her. Radiant as she was in her youth and beauty, the most lovable side of her character ever discovered itself in her tender, worshipping affection for him.

In September, 1860, some months before Chase left Ohio, there was unveiled at Cleveland, on the shores of the Lake to which his valor brought fame, a statue of Commodore Perry, many of the States sending deputations to do honor to his memory. At the head of Rhode Island's troops, in the military parade which opened the ceremonies of the day, rode the governor of that State, his alert young figure impressing itself upon all the spectators of the scene. That night, during the ball at the Kennard House which closed the event of the day, Colonel Richard Parsons presented him to Kate Chase. She was twenty years old at the time, and her slender young figure already possessed that beautiful symmetry that later found such unqualified favor in the eyes of Worth, that great modern connoisseur of the proportions of the female figure, drawing from him such commendation as he never accorded to any other woman. In a ball-gown showing the faultless contour of her neck and throat, and the exquisite poise of her lovely head, she was the revelation of a perfection which the human form rarely attains. Hazel eyes, auburn hair, and the marvellous whiteness of skin that usually accompanies this combination, a full, low, broad brow, mobile lips, a small, round chin, and a nose whose suggestion of an upward tilt added its own peculiar touch of piquancy to a face that was altogether charming rather than classically beautiful,—thus to the eye was Kate Chase, whose fame then superseded that of every woman in Ohio, and was shortly to surpass that of every woman of her generation in America. That she should hold the interested attention of not only one but several men for hours at a time was no unusual spectacle to the people among whom her belleship days had dawned early. Governor Sprague's devotion to her, however, on the night that he first met her, because he was a distinguished stranger and a man of prominence in his own State, and because there seemed, perhaps, in the entire situation many of the elements of romance, became at once a subject of interested comment.

The outbreak of the war took him to Washington. Still governor of his State, he had raised a regiment and equipped it at his own expense, for he was a man of immense wealth. His generosity, his patriotism, and his valor at Bull Run, together with his youth and the success of his political career, appealed to the enthusiasm of his countrymen. The news not only that he was to marry, but to marry a woman so universally idolized as was Kate Chase, heightened the effect his achievements had already produced upon the mind of the public. With a delicate sort of beauty and a somewhat clerical appearance that belied his reputation for military prowess, he had at the moment a fame quite equal to that of his bride. Their marriage, which took place at Washington on the 12th of November, 1863, was the social event of that turbulent period. All the details of the ceremony and of the reception which followed it, and which were planned by her, were on a scale of magnificence worthy of the woman whose advent into Washington had marked a new epoch in its social history.

She was the inspiration of the wedding-march composed for the occasion and played by the Marine Band. Under circumstances when a plain woman is an interesting figure, of what moment was not the appearance of one who could not, even on ordinary occasions, enter a church without her presence being in some mysterious way heralded to its remotest recesses so that every head involuntarily turned towards her! To those who beheld her on that day she was the beautiful realization of the ideal bride, and the life opening before her promised every possible happiness. The ceremony was witnessed by many men and women whose names were then household words when the eyes of the whole nation, watching the direction of the war, were fixed on Washington.

The first days of their married life were spent in Rhode Island, where Mr. Sprague built for his bride the beautiful home that was worthy of her lofty conceptions of a magnificent existence, Canonchet. It was one of the first of the palatial homes of that period, and of which this country now possesses so many, and the cost of its construction was unprecedented in the annals of a people incredibly rich in all life's comforts, but with their luxuriant tendencies for the most part still latent.

From the governorship of his State Sprague went into the United States Senate, and Kate Chase appeared in Washington as the wife of the youngest member of that body. The elegance of the new home there over which she presided, her husband's wealth and prominence, her maturer beauty, and the dignity with which she carried a matron's honors, all tended to bring her before the popular imagination in a more enchanting light than even the glories of her girlhood had done.

The birth of her first child, a son, was a matter of national interest, and the press of the day contained lengthy accounts of the dawn of the little life for which fate held in store so forlorn and tragic an ending. His christening robe was as elaborately described as if it had been that of a royal infant, and the figures of the handsome settlement made upon him were widely published.

Chase, however, still loomed the central figure of his daughter's life, for he continued to confide in her and take counsel with her in all that concerned him personally, as well as those measures that hand his name down as that of the greatest Secretary who ever presided in the Treasury Department. He was the intellectual power of Lincoln's cabinet, and though he contributed much to the success of his administration, there was small sympathy between the men personally, and being overruled by the President in some of the details of his department, Chase, in 1864, resigned his position as a member of the cabinet. Donn Piatt, who was one of the many young Ohioans to whom he was a shining example and a high ideal, said of Chase, that though he came in direct and intimate contact with Lincoln for three years, he never appreciated nor understood the man who could clear the heavy atmosphere of a cabinet meeting, called to consider some such stupendous proposition as the emancipation proclamation, by a hearty laugh, induced by the reading of a chapter from Artemus Ward. Lincoln, however, with his keen knowledge of human nature, discerned Chase's character more readily, and justly estimating the judicial qualities of his superior mind, he sent his nomination as Chief Justice of the United States to the Senate. It was immediately and unanimously confirmed by that body, and on the 6th of December, 1864, Chase, already a great man, entered upon the duties of that office, to which, with one exception, no name has given greater renown.

On February 24, 1868, the House of Representatives passed a resolution to impeach the President of the United States. During his trial, which terminated on

May 26 of the same year, the country passed through a storm of violent political passion. Above the roar of an angry people and the threats which assailed him daily from all sections of the country, rose the august presence of the great Chief Justice, hearing but not heeding, feeling but not fearing their sting. Throughout the country there was no name more frequently heard during those days than that of Chase, and in Washington the President himself was not a more prominent figure. He followed his usual custom of walking to the court in the mornings, being frequently accompanied by the daughter who had so often been his companion in days when there had rested upon him no such burden as the grave question then in hand imposed. She forms one of the bright spots in the memory of that dark period, and he often lifted his eyes during the sessions of the court to refresh them with a glimpse of her face, in whose luminous sympathy there was inspiration. She sat in the gallery of the court chamber every day, surrounded always by men whose names go down in history among those of the foremost of their period and country,—Garfield, Conkling, Sherman, Carl Schurz, with Grant, the military idol of the hour, and Greeley, of editorial eminence.

The chief-justiceship of his country is generally supposed to fill the measure of a man's political aspirations. Upon Chase, however, the honors of his office imposed no such quietus, and in 1868 he again came forward for the Presidential nomination. As a Democrat, who had left his party only on the slavery question, he offered himself as a candidate for the nomination of that party. During the convention, which met in New York, Mrs. Sprague, more ably with her maturer mind and greater resources at her command than she had possessed in 1860, endeavored to bring about the realization of that dream of his whole public life. She was the first, however, to recognize the fact that the only platform on which he could secure the nomination asked more than he could honorably grant. Chase, watching the convention from a distance, confirmed her judgment.

Our history furnishes the names of three men whose ungratified ambition for the Presidency robbed them of their motive in life. Chase, however, survived his disappointment longer than either Webster or Blaine. He was, by nature, profoundly religious, and he endeavored to support with Christian heroism a blow whose crushing force undermined his very vitality. In 1870 he suffered a physical collapse, from which, however, stimulated by his remarkable will-power, he rallied so far as to be able to resume his duties on the Supreme Bench.

On March 23, 1871, the younger of his daughters, the child of his third marriage, was married to William Sprague Hoyt, of New York, a cousin of her sister's husband. Her wedding fastened another brilliant memory upon her father's Washington home at Sixth and E Streets. In the drawing-room, to which she had already brought so much fame, Kate Chase again stood beside her father, and their presence on that day constitutes to many people still living at the capital a memory-picture which, with all deference to the bride, yet supersedes all others of that eventful day. He was a magnificent man, over six feet in height, fair as a Saxon in coloring, with a fine head, clearly defined and well-made features, and a noble beauty of countenance; and she, robed in blue velvet of a turquoise tone, that brought out the glorious red-gold of her hair and the hazel of her eyes, with an Elizabethan collar rolling high about her patrician neck, tall, slender, and full of willowy grace. Perhaps the picture abides because it was the last before the falling of those lengthening shadows whence neither ever emerged.

On the 4th of March, 1873, Chase administered the oath of office to President Grant, and in May of the same year he occupied his chair as Chief Justice for the last time. A few days before the last on which he had felt able to go to court, his daughters and his grandchildren, whom he was accustomed to have much with him, being away from him, a sudden sense of loneliness, a yearning for some loving human presence, seems to have overpowered him, for he wrote to a young relative in New York that he was going to her to be for a while with her and her children. The day after he arrived, however, he went forth quietly and perhaps suddenly on that lonely voyage whence neither love nor the glow of any human presence may withhold us when it comes to be our turn. His body was sent back to Washington, where it arrived on Sunday morning, the 11th of May. There, clad in the awful dignity of death, he lay a day and a night within the bar of the court his living presence had rendered so illustrious. A simple wreath of white rosebuds, not more spotless than the life of him they crowned, was the last offering of the daughter to whom his death, so far as the world knew, brought her first sorrow.

She had, however, already come to the turn in her short road of happiness, and had confronted not alone the spectre of disillusion, which in itself would have been formidable enough to a woman of her temperament, but a substantial form of unhappiness that neither her pride nor a brave spirit that never quailed before it could long conceal. Her life has been so probed, so bared to the scrutiny of the world, that but little of its sorrow can be left to conjecture. That in one of her own deficiencies lay undoubtedly the cause of much of her unhappiness, while it served to render others less culpable, in no degree lessened the force of the misery it entailed upon her.

A knowledge of the proper value of money, abnormally developed in many, was totally lacking in Kate Chase. It appealed to her simply as a means of gratifying the needs and wishes of the moment, never as something to be hoarded for the satisfying of those of a future time. History contains the names of many men and women otherwise illustrious but born apparently with the same defect. The great wealth which came to her through her marriage she expended lavishly, not alone upon herself, but upon all whose happiness it was thus in her power to augment, for such princely natures are rarely selfish. She gave, all her life, frequently with a generosity wholly out of proportion to her means. Sprague probably did not realize her munificent tendencies till after the shrinkage in his fortune caused by the financial panic of the early seventies. They then became the cause of those fatal misunderstandings whence sprung later conditions of insupportable wretchedness. A divorce was granted her by the courts of New York, with permission to resume her maiden name, of which she availed herself some years later, when Sprague married again.

With her three daughters she retired to " Edgewood," a suburban home on the hills two miles north of Washington, which had come to her from her father and which is closely identified with the last years of both their lives. The house, an ample unadorned brick structure, stands on the brow of a hill overlooking the river, the city, and other hills in its vicinity. From her father she had also inherited an income somewhat smaller than might have been anticipated, for, although he had piloted the nation through the financial difficulties of the war, his personal finances were not flourishing. She found a legal adviser in a friend of her father's who had been a frequent visitor at Edgewood during Chase's lifetime, attracted thither both by his admiration for Chase and by the pleasure of that intercourse with his gifted daughter which he shared in common with many men of brilliant minds, few of whom ever came in contact with her without succumbing to a species of intellectual infatuation. With all the feminine graces that attract, however, she had many of a man's characteristics, and was capable of maintaining their intercourse at all times on an intellectual footing. The idle gossip of people who had no conception of the true loftiness of her soul, magnified by those who still felt and feared her political power, cast its blight upon her life. Silently scorning a world that so cruelly misinterpreted her, she voluntarily abandoned her place in its midst.

She took her children to Europe and there educated them, remaining as long as her resources would permit. When they were exhausted she came home. Edgewood gave her a sorry welcome. Everywhere, within and without, it showed signs of long neglect. Yet such as it was, it was home and full of memories of her father, whose portrait still hung in its broad hallway, and whose marble bust still adorned its library. There, too, were his beloved books that he had craved in his youth when he had turned from nature, which became, however, the tender solace of his ailing years, when he liked to be alone with her and his own thoughts, while he took long tramps over the hills. There, during the last three years of his life, he had pursued conscientiously that tranquil existence which he realized could alone prolong his days. To his daughter it was all that remained, and even it was slipping from her grasp. The men of her father's generation were gone, and she was as a stranger in the land that had once resounded with the echo of her name.

Edgewood was advertised for public sale. Something of its history crept into the press of the country.

It struck a chord of memory and appealed to a class of men who had the means of gratifying their sympathies, men of a younger generation, but who venerated the memory of Chase and gave substantial proof of their veneration when they saved his home for the daughter he had so idolized.

She never evinced any desire to resume her place in that life in which she had once been a motive power.

Among those who knew her best she had loyal friends who loved and admired her to the end. Her servants had always worshipped her, and her own children frequently lost themselves in the spell her presence wrought.

Her eldest daughter went upon the stage, but married shortly after her *début* and abandoned whatever hopes she may have had of a histrionic career.

It was a singular fate that the last days in the life of a woman whose youth had scarcely known a moment's exemption from the pursuit of an admiring world should have been passed almost exclusively in the society of the gentle daughter, whom she ever lovingly called her little Kitty.

Two loyal canine friends followed in her footsteps to the last, studying all her movements with a vigilance that was not without its measure of flattery, and receiving from her a degree of consideration that she never failed to show to those of lowly condition in whom she recognized merit not always visible to a more conventional eye. Often the only sound about the lonely house that greeted an occasional visitor, was the friendly thump of the collie's tail against the porch floor, the shrill tone of inquiry in Chiffon's bark, or the melancholy wail of a violin. When Edgewood was finally closed and abandoned after Kate Chase's death, new homes were found for her two dog friends: for the collie, at Brookland, a suburb of Washington, and for the terrier, in the city itself. A few days later both had disappeared, and a boy who had occasion to go to Edgewood found them on the porch of the deserted house. It had been a long tramp for them, especially for the little terrier, which had had to thread its way across the city. Buoyed up with hope, they had arrived from their opposite directions only to realize that a life which at least had been happy for them, had come to its end.

With that rare courage with which she had borne all the other ills of her life, Kate Chase endured uncomplainingly the physical sufferings which its closing days brought to her, endeavoring at first to put them from her and with an aching body to go on heroically with her daily life as she had often done with an aching heart. She surrendered only a few days before the end, realizing then the unusual gravity of her condition, and in the small hours of the morning of the 31st of July, 1899, with her three daughters beside her, she at length closed her tired eyes tranquilly and without fear, to open them never again upon a world that had long since forgotten the once-cherished name of Kate Chase.

For the last few hours yet to be passed beneath the roof of Edgewood, they laid her in the room wherein her life had centred in both its glad and sad days,—her father's library. Its windows overlooked in the foreground the garden in which she had spent of late so many lonely hours, and in the distance, lying beneath the spell of a summer's day, the beautiful city, where regnant woman never held greater sway than she in whose quiet face there was now no trace either of the triumphs or the weariness of her life, but the contentment of grateful rest.

MATTIE OULD

(MRS. OLIVER SCHOOLCRAFT)

IN the vicinity of one of Richmond's fashionable schools there was often seen on winter afternoons, in the late sixties, a group of young girls, who possessed far more than the usual attractiveness that belongs ever to health and youth. Two, at least, Lizzie Cabell and Mary Triplett, were singularly beautiful. The third, a tall, slender girl, with a trim figure, dark skin and hair, and eyes perhaps downcast as she stepped lightly along listening to her companions, a stranger would scarcely have observed. If, perchance, however, as they paused on a street corner for a last word before separating, the downcast eyes were lifted, there gazed from out their soft depths a spirit that transformed the entire face. They were truly the windows of a soul, looking out upon the world with a frankness that was irresistible, and with a certain caressing fondness for life that begot a kindred glow in all it looked upon. In her sweet voice there was the same tone of caress as it gave a parting utterance to some flashing thought to which, likely as not, she paid the tribute of that honest smile, whose witchery still lingers in many minds. As she continued her walk homeward many lifted hats greeted her passing, many eyes followed her, and her name was murmured among many groups, for, young as she was, Mattie Ould was already wandering in the pathway of a fame that was to make her later the idol of the people of the South.

Before she was beyond the tutelage of her old mammy the piquancy of her wit had established her title to popularity. It had, moreover, much of that audacity that had characterized the wit of another Virginia belle, Ann Carmichael, of Fredericksburg, who flourished fifty years earlier in the century. Conventionality was a term with which Mattie Ould had no concern. She was a genius, and with a spontaneity that was overwhelming she dared to give utterance to every sparkling thought that crossed her mind. She was a very small girl when she made that bright sally which connects her name with that of her father's friend, General Young.

A famous *raconteur* and *bon vivant*, and revelling in her gift for repartee, her father frequently had her brought forward as a little child to grace his stag dinners, seating her in the centre of the table, whence she sent forth such sallies of wit as captivated many a veteran dinner-giver and guest.

One evening, when she had kept up her amusing prattle until a later hour than usual, she went up to General Young, who was seated near her father, and stood beside him, resting her head against his shoulder. "Come, come," called her father, "it's time mammy was hunting you up, little sleepy head. General

Young can't get on very well with you there." "No, no," insisted Mattie, dreading a summons of that auto-crat, in whose presence there could be neither pleading nor protest; "don't send for mammy. I'm not sleepy. I was just trying an old head on young shoulders." She was quoted through all grades of Richmond life, and long before she had grown to womanhood a fre-quent question on many lips was, "Have you heard what Mattie Ould said?" Then every one listened to her latest *bon mot*, which was repeated till the whole city had heard and laughed. With a dash and *esprit* that were peculiarly her own, she had many masculine traits, an independence and a *camaraderie* that were irre-sistible.

With the magnetism of her gifts she would have been known to fame even had her family been of less prominence. Well placed, however, as she was in life, her brilliancy illumined a vast horizon. Her father, Judge Robert Ould, always held a distinguished posi-tion, both in the District of Columbia, where he was born, and in Richmond, whither he removed at the out-break of the war. Besides being thrown in intimate con-tact with the prominent citizens of both places, he was frequently called upon to extend his hospitality to emi-nent strangers who came to him with letters of intro-duction. His home during part of his residence in Washington was in the quaint old building opposite the Treasury Department, now Riggs Bank. There President Buchanan was his guest for several days after he quitted the White House. No extraordinary prep-

Mattie Ould
(Mrs. Oliver Schoolcraft)
From photograph by George S. Cook

arations, however, were made for the entertainment of the ex-President in a household where distinguished guests were a frequent occurrence. A loose rod in the stair-carpet was secured on the suggestion of Mrs. Ould's mother, lest Mr. Buchanan, not accustomed to the circumnavigation that it had imposed upon the family, should fall and break his leg, in which event they would have him three weeks instead of three days.

Judge Ould came prominently before the public as the district attorney at the time of the prosecution of General Daniel Sickles for the killing of Barton Key, Sickles being defended by Edwin M. Stanton, who became more widely known later as Lincoln's Secretary of War.

Ould's prominence was rather augmented after the outbreak of the war and his removal to Richmond, where he was made commissioner of the Confederate government for the exchange of prisoners. He had married a celebrated Virginia beauty, Miss Sarah Turpin, and had four children, all of whom, with one noted exception, are still living. His wife, after having been long an invalid, died before his family was grown, and he, some years later, married Mrs. Handy, of Baltimore, the mother of the beautiful May Handy, one of Richmond's belles of the present day.

Mattie Ould was born in the District of Columbia, which she left in her childhood for the home with which her fame is associated. She returned, however, to spend the last two years of her school life in the Visitation Convent, Georgetown. Though known to all

Richmond from her childhood, her renown throughout the South dates from her first appearance at the White Sulphur Springs, which in her day, before the advent of the Northern pleasure-seeker, still possessed all the distinctive features of a Southern watering-place. Though it was already a long-established resort, to the magic which her presence shed about it during the seasons that she spent there it owes much of its wide fame to-day. All the details of the war were then yet vivid memories, and there many a battle was fought over again in graphic words by men whose bravery and gallantry in action have never been surpassed. Many of them had been distinguished officers in the army of the Confederacy,—Joe Johnston, of Virginia; Wade Hampton, of South Carolina; Gordon, of Georgia; Beauregard, of Louisiana; Butler, Gary, the gallant Pickett, of Gettysburg fame; and Hood, of Alabama, then lifting himself about on his crutches. It was such men as these who stamped their striking individuality upon the life of the Southern watering-places at that period, and among whom, keenly appreciating the wit, ardently loving the beauty, and reverencing the goodness of a woman beyond all things, Mattie Ould came to be the greatest belle the South has had since the war.

While she was ever superlatively attractive to men, she was yet a generous friend to women, and frequently avenged the slights to which she saw some plain woman subjected, for, besides the scintillating qualities that made her a popular idol she had many

Lizzie Cabell
(Mrs. Albert Ritchie)

noble traits that commended her to a more profound and lasting admiration.

The toast which is more celebrated than any of her other equally clever utterances was offered at a supper at the Springs, given in honor of herself and another famous Richmond belle, Mary Triplett, the late Mrs. Philip Haxall. Miss Triplett had been asked to propose a toast and had declined. Mattie Ould, however, rose without hesitation, lifted her glass, inclined her graceful head towards Miss Triplett, and in her clear musical voice, said, " Here's to beauty, grace, and wit, which united make a Triplett." There was, indeed, a peculiar enchantment about all she did and said that seemed never to have belonged to any one else. Her dancing infused a new charm into the atmosphere of a ball-room, and as a horsewoman she possessed a skill and grace that few could rival.

Her horse once ran away with her in Richmond, just as the groom mounted her and before she had put her foot in the stirrup. It dashed off at top speed, running several squares through the residence district of the city, and then turned into a business street, where it rushed madly into a hack. The hackman, however, had seen it coming, and realizing that he could not get out of its way, he stood up, and throwing his arm around the rder's waist, he lifted her from the saddle as the horse crashed into the hack, partly demolishing it, and fell. A great crowd witnessed the rescue, and cheered lustily for the courageous old hackman. When Mattie Ould was recognized, however, the enthusiasm assumed a more substantial form, and the hands of many men went generously into their pockets. He was never forgotten, and as long as Mattie Ould lived she provided for him and his family, some of the many who had loved her keeping up the good work after she was gone.

Though she was the object of the ardent devotion of many men, she did not marry until she had passed her twenty-fifth year. It was rumored that she was engaged to a friend of her father's, a man many years her senior, and the indignation with which her father received the news of her marriage to Oliver Schoolcraft substantiated in many minds the report of the former engagement.

Her marriage occurred at the end of the summer of 1876, which she had spent with her grandmother at the White Sulphur Springs. Thither Schoolcraft, one of the wealthiest of the younger set of men who adorned Richmond life, had followed her, taking with him his own valuable horses and traps, with which adjuncts he was ever at her disposal. They drove over to Salem one day, and were quietly married there that evening, at the home of Mr. and Mrs. John A. McCall; one of Miss Ould's brothers and several of her friends witnessing the ceremony. As no preparation had been made for her marriage, she wore, instead of the conventional white satin, a simple gown of white organdy, set off with bands of black velvet.

She was never more bewitchingly lovely than she was that night, and so impressed herself indelibly on the minds of all who gathered about her, some of

Mary Triplett
(Mrs. Philip Haxall)
From photograph by Roseti

whom were but little children. Being asked to sing in the course of the evening, she complied with her usual graciousness, for part of the charm of her manner lay not only in her readiness to contribute to the pleasure of others, but in the absolute enjoyment she evinced in so doing. She made her own selection, and sang the little song that was then in favor with her, " Under the Daisies." It was singularly prophetic, for just as the daisies of another spring were putting forth their bloom the sweet voice, whose vibrations had rung so many glad echoes from the world, lapsed forever into silence.

Schoolcraft took her to Richmond the day following their marriage, where her father insisted upon having the ceremony performed again, owing to some technicality of the law to the effect that a marriage license should be obtained at the usual place of residence of the bride. Though the spirit of comradeship had existed to an unusual degree between this father and daughter, he never forgave her until it was too late for that forgiveness to be any comfort to her.

She lived, after her marriage, in an elegant suite of rooms, built over Schoolcraft's handsomely equipped stables. When some one twitted her about the peculiar location of her new abode, she replied, with her unfailing readiness, that she was not the first person who had lived in a stable, and quoted a precedent that no Christian could gainsay.

One morning, in the spring following her marriage, Richmond was appalled by the report which, in the course of a few hours had spread over the entire city, that Mattie Ould was dying. The world was so full of her and all she did and said, that it was not credible that her beguiling presence was passing from it. A silent depression and a sense of personal loss settled upon the people in every walk of life.

Richmond had never beheld such a sight as Mattie Ould's funeral. Old St. Paul's Church and the Square opposite were thronged, the streets all along the route to the cemetery were lined, and even the hills of beautiful Hollywood were black with people. The entire population of the city was there, many, who were too poor to ride, walking, for she had brightened all their lives, and she belonged to them all.

She lies all through the spring and summer beneath a bed of daisies, and near her sleeps the infant whose life closed her own. In the memory of the people of the South she is yet a living presence, whose words, wise and droll, are repeated, ever with a keen relish for their pungency, for she touched all things with that true wit which is

> " Nature to advantage dressed,
> What oft before was thought,
> But ne'er so well expressed."

JENNIE JEROME

(LADY RANDOLPH CHURCHILL)

TO-DAY, when there are so many American women adorning high places and filling more or less leading *rôles* in British society, it is difficult to realize that only a little more than a quarter of a century ago there was a strong movement afoot, among certain leaders of that society, to exclude their fair transatlantic cousins from London drawing-rooms. As to the oft-recurring Anglo-American marriage, while there are yet many people who look askance upon any sort of an international alliance, that prejudice that frowned so ominously upon it some years ago has wonderfully abated on both sides of the water. The Queen herself recently confessed that she had regarded it at one time as rather a hazardous experiment, but realizing that, with her broad education and elastic temperament, the American girl adapts herself to a new environment with a facility which would scarcely be possible to the less flexible English girl, Her Majesty's apprehensions have been gradually allayed.

One of the first American women before whom these later-day barriers of social prejudice gave way was Miss Jennie Jerome, of New York. As the wife of Lord

Randolph Churchill, and ably championed by his mother the Duchess of Marlborough, she penetrated the innermost recesses of British society, opening the way more than any other woman to the position her countrywomen occupy there at the end of the century, and holding herself a place second to that of no other American woman in Europe.

The admiration she attracted as a young girl, the wonderful part she played in the life of her husband and is at present playing in the lives of her sons, the unusual influence she has undeniably exercised in English politics, the intimate contact into which the events of her life have from time to time thrown her with the crowned heads of Europe,—the Czar of Russia, the Emperor of Germany, and the Queen of England,—have all tended to give her a unique place in the history of the latter days of the Victorian era. In England there is no woman below the royal family whose name and personality are so generally known as Lady Randolph Churchill's.

Her prominent identification with the Primrose League has carried her fame into the colonies and into India. Many people in Russia and Germany follow her career with keen interest, the press of both countries bringing her frequently before the public, and even in self-centred France the women of the aristocracy, in imitation of her political achievements, have from time to time essayed to "jouer la Lady Randolph Churchill."

She is the eldest of three daughters of the late Mr.

JENNIE JEROME

Leonard Jerome, and was born in Brooklyn, on the 9th of January, 1854. There and in New York she passed her early childhood.

Her mother was a woman of independent fortune and her father an enterprising and successful man of affairs. He was the founder, in New York, of the Jockey Club, and his name figures conspicuously in the annals of the turf of both England and America, he having been one of its active patrons in the former country, whose racing system he introduced into America.

His family migrated to Paris when his eldest daughter was in her eleventh year, and there his children grew up and were educated. Miss Jennie Jerome's artistic and musical gifts were carefully trained, and she has been considered ever since she made her *entrée* into English society as one of its most accomplished pianists. Her name appears frequently on the programmes of concerts given in behalf of charity, and is always a powerful drawing card, for she plays with a clearness and delicacy of touch rarely attained by an amateur.

France was at the height of its glories under the second empire when the Jeromes took up their residence in Paris. The court, presided over by one of the most beautiful women who ever wore a diadem, was characterized by almost unprecedented magnificence. Paris then, as now, led the world in all matters of personal adornment, and one feature in that *régime* of luxuriant display, inaugurated by the Empress, is still felt to-day in every quarter of the globe where women make any pretence of following fashions in dress. She never permitted any woman to appear twice in her presence in the same gown. As a result, there dates from her brief era of leadership an extravagance in woman's dress that was before undreamed of, and which has had the effect of raising the details of a toilet from a subordinate to a ruling position among women in fashionable life, with a loss of much that gave a truer beauty to existence under a system when the sparkle of a woman's mind was of greater value than the flash of her jewels.

Mrs. Jerome, a woman of wealth and taste, easily acquired a position of distinction in the fashionable life of the French capital at that time. Her eldest daughter meanwhile grew up with a reputation for great beauty, her fame increasing as the unusual gifts of her bright mind unfolded themselves. She was one of that group of clever and beautiful young girls with whom the Emperor and Empress from time to time surrounded the little Prince Imperial, and she participated at Compiègne in the memorable celebration of one of the few birthday anniversaries which fate accorded him,

The Franco-Prussian war drove the Jeromes across the channel. They tarried in England during the days that marked the fall of the empire and the uprising of the Communards with their awful deeds of devastation. The summer of 1873 they passed at Cowes.

Miss Jennie Jerome was then in her twentieth year, tall, slender, with a thoughtful countenance denoting both talent and character in its broad brow and square chin. Her mouth was grave and sweet, while her great dark eyes, that are yet the most striking feature of her face, her purple black hair, and her clear olive skin gave her a distinctive place among the blonde daughters of England. Always a striking figure in their midst, the contrast was perhaps never more marked than upon the occasion of the marriage of Princess Louise of Wales to the Earl of Fife, when the blonde type of the British women was so much in evidence in the demi-toilettes commanded by the Queen, and when Lady Randolph Churchill's brunette coloring was so well set off by her yellow satin gown, with a diamond star twinkling above her brow against her black hair.

Though the nomadic tendency of Americans frequently leads them abroad, where they mingle for awhile in the life of various European capitals, there were fewer American women at that time forming a permanent part of foreign society, and one so gifted mentally and physically as was Miss Jerome soon became a noted figure. She attracted everywhere the most evident admiration, never impairing the effect her appearance produced by the least manifestation of vanity.

To the Isle of Wight also that summer there betook himself a young English nobleman, the second son of the sixth Duke of Marlborough. But three years out of college, where he had not been distinguished as a student, but rather for the irresistible attractiveness of his personality and for the enjoyment he extracted from existence, there was little in Lord

Randolph Churchill's life in the summer of 1873 that foreshadowed the greatness he was destined to attain. Restless, ambitious, full of energy, with no specific object upon which to expend it, he hesitated between a diplomatic and a military career, and meanwhile, since taking his degree in 1871, he had travelled over the whole of Europe.

He was already an idol to his mother, towards whom he ever showed that thoughtfulness that is the acme of gallantry. He had much of her dash and spirit, and she entered sympathetically into all the events of his life; he on his side never failing to report to her immediately, either in person or by message, all his successes. When he met Jennie Jerome, and for the first time the future assumed a tangible and very beautiful form, he confided in his mother and at once solicited her interest in the young American girl.

To Miss Jerome's mother, however, Lord Randolph Churchill, a younger son, with no particularly bright prospects in life, did not appeal as a desirable match. She returned to Paris with her daughters. Lord Randolph followed, and there at the British Embassy, in January, 1874, he was married to Miss Jerome.

With an ambition and talent equal to his own, she entered completely into his desire to make for himself a place of distinction in life. The dissolution of Parliament early in the year of his marriage offered the opportunity for a political career. He began at home, in the borough of Woodstock, in which Blenheim Palace, where he had been born twenty-five years

Jennie Jerome
(Lady Randolph Churchill)
From photograph by Van der Weyde

before, is situated, and secured his election to a seat in the House of Commons without being asked any questions as to his political creed, which, it was taken for granted, was identical with that of his family.

Like his wife's father, he took an active interest in matters pertaining to the turf, owning several famous race-horses and capturing during the course of his life some notable prizes. His first speech in Parliament was to call the attention of the first Commissioner of Public Works to the hard and dusty condition of Rotten Row, and to ask that it be put in better shape, without delay, for both horses and their riders.

During the first six almost silent years of his Parliamentary career, while he was studying the men and measures he subsequently arraigned with so much brilliancy, his young wife was adapting herself to the social life of his country, whose events are as well established as those of its political life. In a dutiful way which gives it a dignity not possible in a country whose social usages admit of more caprice, every one lives up to the well-appointed order in which, beginning with the first drawing-room in the early spring, the various functions of each season follow one another.

While there may be more refreshment and enthusiasm in the novelty which American society admits of, it lacks that stability that emanates from the very sameness with which one English year follows in the footsteps of another, and that sense of ancient respectability which rises from the consciousness of participating in the same pleasures from youth to old age in which one's fathers similarly participated in their time.

Lady Randolph Churchill easily overcame the prejudices which existed in the minds of some English women against all American women. Young as she was, there was a commanding quality in her very presence which vanquished that narrowness that harbors petty dislike on a basis of nationality.

Both of her sisters married in England, one to Moreton Frewen and the other to the only son of Sir John Leslie, Bart., of Glaslough Monaghan.

Her two sons were born, the first, Winston Spencer Churchill, on the 30th of November, 1874, and the younger, John Winston Churchill, in February, 1880.

Between the duties of her home and those of a social nature, which her position in the world entailed upon her, the first period of her life in England passed. From 1880, however, dated the dramatic period of Lord Randolph Churchill's career, in which his wife bore so conspicuous a part. He rose to the leadership of that small section of the House known as the "Fourth Party," which, coming forward as an evidence of the vigor yet possessed by the Conservatives, succeeded in June, 1885, in overthrowing the Gladstonian ministry. He was frequently compared to Disraeli, and many people prophesied for him a similar career.

In 1883, in connection with Sir H. Drummond Wolf, Lord Randolph Churchill founded, in the interests of the Conservative party, that powerful organization, the Primrose League. In a membership to-day of over one and a half million, with Knights, Dames, and Associates, Lady Randolph Churchill stands number twelve upon its rolls. The kingdom and empire of Great Britain are dotted with its Habitations.

With its development there began a new phase of Lady Churchill's life. She became from that moment thoroughly an Englishwoman, identifying herself closely with her husband's public life and interests, aiding him not only with the popularity she had already attained, but with the remarkable sagacity she displayed in reference to all political questions. With the qualities that rendered her more charming as a woman she combined those most valuable in a man. Ambitious, intrepid, discreet, she was yet graceful, tactful, wise, and witty. She became at once a force among the members of the League, and, besides being much in demand at the social events at its various Habitations, she endeavored continually to impress upon its members the influence each might exercise in behalf of " that party which is pledged to support all that is dear to England, Religion, Law, Order, and Unity of the Empire."

In her character of Dame of the Primrose League she has participated in so many electioneering contests that she is almost as well known in England as any man in public life. When her husband, in 1885, attacked the seat held by Mr. John Bright for Birmingham, seconded by the Duchess of Marlborough, she canvassed the constituency for him. Never before had women gone thus among the workingmen of Birmingham, entering the factories as well as their homes, and addressing them both collectively and individually. Though they made much havoc in the ranks of Radicalism and greatly diminished his votes, they did not succeed in defeating "the tribune of the people."

Lady Churchill is a rousing speaker, and, with her great beauty and magnetism, evoked immense enthusiasm, her carriage being frequently surrounded and followed for some distance by cheering crowds. In South Paddington her efforts told with better effect, Lord Churchill securing the election in that district.

With the accession to office of Lord Salisbury's government, Lord Churchill went into the Cabinet as Secretary of State for India,—the real head of affairs of the far-away empire where the power is represented by a governor-general. During his brief tenure of that office his wife was decorated with the imperial order of the Crown of India, which has so recently been bestowed upon another American woman in the person of the present governor-general's wife.

Lord Churchill stood at this time at the very head of his party, and when a few months after resigning the office as Secretary of State for India he again went into the Cabinet as Chancellor of the Exchequer and leader of the House of Commons, being at the time but thirty-seven years of age, there seemed opening to him a future of almost unprecedented brilliancy. More than ever was it said that he was treading in the footsteps of Lord Beaconsfield, to whom he had been so often compared, and the Prime Ministership seemed almost within his reach. His name was on every tongue, and when he appeared in public places accompanied by his wife, whose tall, slender figure and clear-eyed, interested face were as well known as his own, he was frequently greeted with outbursts of applause. When she drove in Hyde Park her carriage was frequently followed, and she was pointed out with the most enthusiastic admiration.

Not only in England, but accompanying her husband to Russia and Germany, she excited in both of those countries a similar sentiment, there being among the people an eager desire to see the beautiful American who was so much admired by the court circles.

Attractive as she was under all circumstances, she never more admirably reflected the fine qualities of her character than on that day when her husband rose amidst the absolute silence of the House of Commons to give his reasons for withdrawing from the Cabinet. Absorbed in him, she followed intently his every word and gesture, though aware beforehand of every syllable he would utter. With perfect self-control she revealed nothing either of regret, disappointment, or any sentiment upon which a guess at his plans for the future might be hazarded.

Socially her life ran in much the same channel. So great was her beauty and so many were her talents that, though her husband gradually withdrew from public life, she was continually in the public eye, being constantly in demand to open fairs, distribute prizes, and take part in concerts. In March, 1888, she went to

Clydebank to christen the "City of New York," at that time one of the most remarkable vessels that had been built. During the following summer she opened an electrical exhibit at Birmingham, and a few days later conferred the annual awards at Malvern College, her husband accompanying her and making addresses upon both occasions. About this time also she made her first appearance as a *literata* in an article on the social life of Russia, based on the observations she had made while in St. Petersburg with her husband. Well informed, keenly observant, clever, and witty, she entered the lists without handicap, and her position to-day in the world of letters is at least unique. The most costly quarterly in existence, now entering upon its second year, is owned and edited by her.

In 1891, when he was but forty-two years old, Lord Randolph Churchill came suddenly face to face with the beginning of the end of his remarkable and crowded life. The utter physical collapse that followed, terminating in death in January, 1895, threw light upon much that had seemed inexplicable in the latter days of his public career.

Accompanied by his wife, he journeyed around the world in quest of the health which he was destined never to find. They passed through New York, Lady Churchill's first home, but made no stay, hastening across the continent to San Francisco. In Egypt, realizing how futile had been the long days and nights of travel and exile, he begged to be taken home to pass there the last few hours that yet remained to him.

JENNIE JEROME

From all who saw them they evoked pity and admiration,—pity for the man, stricken and doomed, in the very prime of his days and with the highest place among the statesmen of his time almost within his grasp, and admiration for the wife who, aglow with beauty, spirit, and ambition, manifested for him during those months of tragic gloom, in which his life closed, all the devotion and admiration which the most successful moments of his life, when he stood on the very pinnacle of fame, had called forth from her gratified heart.

The untimely disappearance from the world of a man whose magnetic nature had made him a leader of men and an idol of all classes of society appealed powerfully to public feeling. The tolling of the funeral bell from St. George's, in Hanover Square, a little after noon on the 24th of January, 1895, announced his death.

Though she took no part in the doings of the world for some time after her husband's death, Lady Randolph Churchill did not drop from its memory, nor is she in any degree less interesting to-day than she was as the wife of an eminent statesman. Her musical gifts and tastes gradually drew her from the seclusion of her early widowhood, and she reappeared in public first at concerts and at the opera, still dressing in black.

Her social graces and talents make her the genius of many house-parties, where individual gifts and accomplishments show to best advantage and are most in demand. In the tableaux and burlesque given at Blenheim Palace in January, 1898, to raise money for the

Restoration Fund of St. Mary Magdalene's church at Woodstock, she appeared as a lady journalist, portraying the character with a realism that manifested an accurate knowledge of the original. She was also a guest at Chatsworth House during a recent visit of the Prince and Princess of Wales, taking part there in the private theatricals which were part of the entertainment offered to their Royal Highnesses.

To her sons she is a congenial spirit, being interested in the things that interest them, particularly in yachting, horses, and the various racing events of each year. It is owing largely, no doubt, to her love of an active out-of-door life that her figure yet retains much of the slenderness and suppleness of young womanhood. She stands and walks with all the grace of a girl, and is one of the most noted skaters in England.

Not only into their recreations, but into the serious side of her sons' lives, she enters with that earnestness which made her so inseparable a part of her husband's life.

In the summer of 1899 the elder of her sons, Mr. Winston Churchill, made his first effort for a seat in Parliament. Oldham, in Lancashire, the scene of his endeavors, has two Parliamentary seats, which both became vacant at the same time. Though they had been filled by Conservatives, the result of the balloting in 1899 showed that the cotton-spinners, who form a large class of the voters of the borough, were tired of Conservative rule, for both Liberal candidates came in with heavy majorities.

JENNIE JEROME

Towards the end of the campaign Lady Randolph Churchill went vigorously and enthusiastically to her son's assistance. "The Liberal candidates being married," she said, "have an advantage." Though she won him many votes and greatly reduced the opposition, as she had done in the days of the Birmingham contest, when her husband attacked Bright's seat, the result was inevitable, and both mother and son accepted it with the grace and spirit of thoroughbred woman- and manhood.

There is an anecdote frequently related of Lady Churchill's ready wit, called forth by a situation which arose during the electioneering campaign, in which she was taking an active interest, of Mr. Burdett-Coutts, husband of the old Baroness Burdett-Coutts, who was at the time over eighty years of age. An old voter upon whom Lady Churchill called, and who seemed ready enough to cast his vote for Mr. Burdett-Coutts, took occasion, however, to relate to her, with much relish, the price which the beautiful Duchess of Devonshire had paid a butcher for his vote in the days of the famous Pitt and Fox contest, permitting him to kiss her lovely cheek. He concluded his narration with a direct intimation that he would consider a similar reward as fair payment for his own vote.

"Very well," replied Lady Churchill, smiling a gracious compliance, "I will book your vote on those terms, but you must remember that I am working for Mr. Burdett-Coutts, and I must, therefore, refer you for payment to the Baroness."

In June, 1899, the first number of Lady Churchill's quarterly, the *Anglo-Saxon Review*, which had been for several months the subject of much conjecture and speculation, appeared.

> ' Have you heard of the wonderful new magazine
> Lady Randolph's to edit with help from the Queen ?
> It's a guinea a number—too little by half,
> For the crowned heads of Europe are all on the staff,''

ran the opening lines of perhaps the cleverest of the many verses and paragraphs her new venture called forth.

Its contributions included papers from Lord Rose-berry and Whitelaw Reid, a poem from Swinburne, with stories from Henry James, Gilbert Parker, and Sir Frank Sweetenham, and a drama from John Oliver Hobbes. Among the illustrations were a picture of the Queen, as frontispiece, and a reproduction of Gilbert Stewart's portrait of Washington. The binding was in keeping with the contents, and was of dark-blue morocco, richly tooled in gold, with the royal coat of arms in the centre, surmounted by the crown of England, with supporters, a reproduction of a cover designed in the seventeenth century by the court binder, Abraham Bateman. It sold, as have the subsequent editions, for a guinea a number, and was, as the enterprising editress said in her preface, a volume " worthy to be taken up into that Valhalla of printed things, the library."

At the outbreak of the war in the Transvaal in 1899 Lady Randolph Churchill gave another evidence of her public spirit and enterprise which identified her once again with her native country. As chairman of the committee of the American hospital ship " Maine," she took an active part in the direction and equipment of one of the finest ambulance ships in the service. The ship itself was loaned by the Atlantic Transport Company, and named in memory of the ill-fated American battle-ship " Maine." The contributions for its equipment were made by Americans on both sides of the ocean. Among the American women living in England who actively interested themselves in the matter were Mrs. Joseph Chamberlain, Mrs. Arthur Paget, Mrs. Bradley-Martin, and both of Lady Randolph Churchill's sisters.

An appeal, issued on the 27th of October, for thirty thousand pounds met with a speedy response, and in the course of a few weeks the American hospital ship " Maine," flying the flag that was a gift from the Queen, and with accommodations for two hundred sick or wounded soldiers, carrying its corps of surgeons and nurses and Lady Randolph Churchill herself, was on its way to Durban.

Though it was as the wife of Lord Randolph Churchill and through her close identification with his interests that Lady Churchill first came prominently before the world, it is undoubtedly her own personality that has made for her the place she holds there to-day.

On the 28th of July, 1900, Lady Randolph Churchill became the wife of Mr. George Cornwallis West. Though marriages of women to men many years their junior are by no means rare in British society, the rumor of this engagement, which had been afloat for quite a year, excited an unusual amount of comment and criticism. The ceremony was performed at St. Paul's Church, Knightsbridge, the Duke of Marlborough leading Lady Churchill to the altar. Though widows of titled men in England may upon entering into a second marriage retain the name and title acquired through their former marriage, Lady Randolph Churchill settled the much-discussed question as to whether she would retain hers by her decision to be known as Mrs. George Cornwallis West.

Not yet in middle life, and with two sons to be launched upon their careers, in which she has already foreshadowed what her part may be, the world may still expect to hear much of her, for there is a bracing and vigorous quality in her individuality that renders her interesting and inspiring to many classes and many countries. She has been frequently reproduced in the fiction of her era, more than one English writer drawing his material continually from her life and character.

To what extent her beauty forms part of her magnetism is with many people a debatable question. Though Long painted her as a typical beauty, and Sargent's canvas of her that hangs in her own library portrays an exquisite feminine loveliness, she leans perhaps too much towards the masculine in mental poise and temperament to be an adequate reflection of purely feminine beauty. A many-sided, strong, self-sustained character, her outward form is an expression of her own uncommon personality rather than a type of conventional beauty.

NELLIE HAZELTINE

(MRS. FREDERICK W. PARAMORE)

AMONG the members of the graduating class at Mary Institute, St. Louis, in the year 1873, was a young girl who, in addition to the bright mind and intellectual ambition she had already manifested, was endowed with so extraordinary a physical beauty and so lovable a character that much of the brilliancy of her life might even then have been foretold. She was not yet seventeen years old, and was as absolutely unconscious of the unusual loveliness of her person as she ever seemed to be even after ten years of adulation.

Her figure had already attained a faultless contour, and in her simple graduation gown of white French muslin, the flounces of its skirt headed with wreaths of pink roses and green leaves, and its round bodice offset with a bertha covered in the same design of roses and leaves, she suggested all the fragrance and beauty of a flower. Her red-gold hair seemed to reflect some of the sun's own glory, and with the marvellous delicacy of her skin, the deep wine-color of her eyes, and the classic perfection of her features, there can be little doubt that she was, as she was so often said to be later, the most beautiful woman ever born west of the Mississippi.

Among her school-mates Nellie Hazeltine had won that popularity that was hers in after years to so remarkable an extent among all women. The power she possessed of diffusing herself and all that pertained to her among others precluded every thought of envy, and those with whom she came in contact experienced rather a sense of personal gratification in the contemplation of her gifts than any desire to despoil her of them or of the admiration they attracted.

She was the only daughter of Captain William B. Hazeltine, a man who had made a large fortune in the mercantile world, and she went from school to further enhance the attractiveness of an already beautiful home. There for several years she continued her studies, though it was not unusual then for girls of her age to take up their position in the social world immediately upon quitting school. As a result her accomplishments were of a higher order than those commonly possessed by the young women of her period. She was well read, she spoke French with the same ease with which she spoke her mother tongue, and was a musician of unusual ability. Such attributes soon gained for her a wide reputation and a unique position in the society of her native city.

In the matter of its social complexion St. Louis has generally been classed among the cities of the South. Besides the French, who formed a large proportion of its early settlers, those who rose early to a leading position were the families who had migrated there from Virginia and Kentucky. They were slave-owners and

Nellie Hazeltine
(Mrs. Frederick W. Paramore)
From photograph by J. C. Strauss

landholders, and as such gave a substantial character to the social foundations of the city. The Anglo-Saxon gradually absorbed the French element, which, though it disappeared from the political horizon, still formed a powerful undercurrent in the lives of the people, harmonizing the forms of their social intercourse and imparting a certain artistic value to their existence generally, that gave St. Louis a distinctive place among the growing and wealthy young cities in its vicinity. This, with the character it took from the dominant race, which restrained it from that tendency to display that was elsewhere more or less apparent, yet which ever inculcated the sacred laws of hospitality, blended into a delightful whole and gave to the city a charm that it has never lost.

Of such a civilization Nellie Hazeltine has unquestionably been the fairest product. Yet no one was less conscious than she of the eminence of her position or of the sensation her appearance invariably created.

Shortly after the beginning of her social career she went with her father to Washington to attend a competitive drill of military organizations from all sections of the country. While there she was selected to present the colors to the company of which her father was captain. Among the spectators of a scene which is always more or less inspiring, was a man who, though already past middle-life, was yet not proof against the witchery of such a singularly lovely presence as Nellie Hazeltine's. From the moment she thus crossed his life, like many another man of less prominence, Samuel

J. Tilden followed her career with an ardent and chivalrous admiration that increased as her beautiful character developed and disclosed itself.

When he came before the country as the Democratic candidate for the Presidency, and captured not only the nomination but the majority vote of the people, when his name was on every tongue in America, and everything that concerned him was of absorbing interest, the story of his devotion to Nellie Hazeltine spread throughout the length and breadth of the country.

From the moment it became known that Samuel J. Tilden had been elected President of the United States, till Samuel J. Randall, Speaker of the House of Representatives, cutting the tie vote of that body, redeemed its pledge to abide by the decision of the Electoral Commission, which declared Rutherford B. Hayes President of the United States, forms one of the most thrilling periods in our political history. It was but eleven years after the great civil struggle, and people living to-day, when the sinews of the nation are again knitted, cannot easily estimate the bitterness engendered by the campaign that fell during our centennial year.

The contest reached nothing less than a sublime climax when Randall, with nothing in his great form or his strong face to betray the struggle it had cost him, stepped quietly down from the Speaker's platform, and, taking his place on the floor of the House, uttered amid its breathless silence that affirmative syllable upon which hung national tranquillity.

Both men took the oath of office,—Tilden, the people's choice, in the privacy of his own home in New York, and Hayes, twice, first, on Saturday afternoon, the 3d of March, in the White House, overlapping Grant's term of office by a few hours, that there might be no intermission occasioned by inauguration-day falling on Sunday; and again on Monday, the 5th of March, in the presence of the people.

A Presidential campaign that proceeds and terminates in the usual way is sufficient to entail an enormous amount of publicity upon the candidates. The campaign of '76, however, gave Tilden both a prominence and a place in the affections of the people of his country that could scarcely have been greater had he been permitted to fill the high office to which they elected him.

His bachelorhood was an interesting feature of his personality, for we had had at that time but one bachelor President. The sentimental side of public opinion was satisfied, however, with the report that he was soon to be married to Miss Hazeltine. On her part, though his admiration for her was easily apparent, she never referred to his having offered himself to her any more than she revealed the fact of any other man ever having honored her with a similar proposal. Yet it was known through men who could not easily disguise the sharpness of their disappointment at her rejection of their suit that she was continually the recipient of such offers.

Though she was already well known socially, in both St. Louis and New York, her fame was established after the summers of 1876 and 1877 on a vastly wider basis.

During the latter season she made a tour of the Eastern watering-places, and went for the first time to the Greenbrier White Sulphur Springs, succeeding Mattie Ould in its social leadership during the last days of the old *régime*, when it occupied the first rank as a distinctively Southern resort.

There was no one who made any pretence of rivalling her, though fair women from every section of the South still upheld the fame of the old resort. She has been frequently compared to Mattie Ould, and the history of their short lives furnishes several points of similarity. Hers was a more faultless type of beauty than Mattie Ould's, however, and she had a reserve and dignity that were in keeping with its high order, whereas, Mattie Ould was distinguished by a flow of spirits and a brilliancy of wit that captivated every fancy and carried all before it. Both had the power to attract and hold the attention and admiration of large circles of people, one by the overwhelming sparkle of her words, the other by the magic of a lovely presence.

Nellie Hazeltine was at all times as charming in the society of her own sex as she was among men; and women in every rank of life had for her a tender attachment. Many a girl trying her uncertain young social wings for the first time owed to her that subsequent enjoyment and happiness which is called success. She was absolutely unselfish, and without display used the remarkable power which her own fascinating personality gave her to add to the happiness or improve the condition of others.

NELLIE HAZELTINE

On the 2d of December, 1881, she was married to Mr. Frederick W. Paramore, a young railroad man of St. Louis, and a son of Mr. J. W. Paramore, who was president of the Texas and St. Louis Railroad.

Memories of her, like those of Mattie Ould, centre in the days of a glorious girlhood. She was but twenty-seven years of age when she passed out of life, a little more than two years after her marriage, followed by an infant son whose existence had measured but a few days. The entire city of St. Louis mourned her loss, and few people have been laid to rest amid such evidences of a profound and universal grief as followed her. Her grave in Bellefontaine, whither strangers visiting St. Louis still frequently make a pilgrimage, was literally filled in with flowers by the young women of the city, to whom her life had been a beautiful example.

In the Museum of St. Louis, there hangs a portrait of her painted by Carl Gutherz. It is a full-length figure dressed in white and standing in her own drawing-room. Her abundant hair is arranged after the peculiar fashion of the day, with a heavy fringe low on the fore-head. From beneath it, however, there looks down upon the beholder a face reflecting something of both the heart and mind whence flowed the charm of Nellie Hazeltine's personality, and of a beauty so ideal as to be almost sufficient in itself to immortalize her among the women of her country.

MARY VICTORIA LEITER

(BARONESS CURZON OF KEDLESTON)

FOR the second time within the century an American woman has risen to viceregal honors. Mary Caton, the granddaughter of Charles Carroll of Carrollton and the widow of Robert Patterson, of Baltimore, through her marriage, in 1825, to the Marquis of Wellesley, who was at the time Viceroy of Ireland, went to reign a queen in the country whence her ancestors, more than a century before, had emigrated to America. In Mary Victoria Leiter, whose life, to the people of a future generation, will read much like romance, we again behold an American woman, who, like the Marchioness of Wellesley at the time she became Vicereine of Ireland, is still young and beautiful, filling a similar position in India, with its four hundred millions of subjects.

The parallel between her life and that of Mary Caton, however, goes no farther. Wellesley was already in possession of the Governor-Generalship of Ireland when he married Mrs. Patterson. He was, moreover, beyond the threescore mark in years, and he bore " his blushing honors thick upon him," having already been Viceroy of India. Curzon was but thirty-nine years old when the governor-generalship of the latter mighty country, the shining mark of many a man's whole career, was offered to him. His public life bore little more than "the tender leaves of hope," though his writings on Eastern topics were already accepted as highly authoritative. Lady Wellesley had but to follow the leadership of a man of recognized ability and established fame, while Lady Curzon walks side by side with the man who is making that steep ascent which the British editorial mind has classified as "Salisbury's most interesting experiment." It is, moreover, an open secret that, far from shrinking from the new office, with the weight of responsibility which it imposed, she encouraged her husband to accept it.

While we are familiar with that phase of international marriage which confers rank and title upon the daughters of our republic, no American woman has ever played such a part in the British empire as has fallen to the lot of Lady Curzon. From that day in the spring of 1895, when she became the wife of the young Commoner, George Nathaniel Curzon, she stepped into English history; the days of her American belleship became a fragrant reminiscence. The qualities which had given them brilliancy, however, continued to illuminate the broader horizon of her life in England, and have become in her present exalted position the admiration of her own country, whose interest in her is purely personal, and the gratification of England, whose interest is political and much farther-reaching.

To the vast majority of people, who have but a superficial knowledge of Lady Curzon, her charm lies in the phases of that exterior life which are visible to all and easily discerned from afar,—her youth, her beauty, her wealth, the artistic perfection of her raiment, and the glory and pageant of her present existence. These, however, are but foot-lights to the real power of the woman rising beyond them.

As a girl in America she stood forth against the rich background of her home as distinctly as she is silhouetted to-day against the magnificence of the throne of India. It was not so much what she did or said, though that was sometimes of an unusual order, that made her the social power she was in America; it was rather what people instinctively felt that she was. "What thou art," says Emerson, defining that force we call character, "so roars and thunders above thy head, I cannot hear thee speak." She was serious and earnest rather than scintillating, with a reserve and dignity of manner tempered by a sweetness that admitted no suggestion of austerity.

The grace with which she now meets every situation, the intelligent interest she manifests in every theme with which she is approached, are not matters of happy chance or accident. She has been carefully equipped for her place in life. Studious and ambitious, she has known little of frivolity or idleness. Every faculty and every gift with which she was endowed have been conscientiously cultivated, so that, like the wise virgins of the parable, she was found ready when the hour came with a light that guides not only her own footsteps, but is seen from afar.

Jennie Chamberlain
(Lady Naylor-Leyland)
From the painting by H. Schmiechen

MARY VICTORIA LEITER

Though Lady Curzon's life has been largely cosmo-
politan, the city of Chicago, in which she was born
and passed her first thirteen years, has a more substantial claim upon her than any in which she has since
lived. She evidently reciprocates the feeling of the
former city, for it was to it that she recently addressed
a plea in behalf of the famine-stricken districts of
India. It was there that her father, Mr. Levi Z. Leiter,
amassed his immense fortune, laying its foundation as
a partner in the dry-goods firm of Marshall Field &
Co. There, also, her brother, Joseph Leiter, still continues his remarkable position in the stock market.

In the year 1881 Lady Curzon's family joined that
ever-increasing colony at Washington that is made up
of wealth and leisure. It has in recent years become
a distinctive feature of the capital, its members having
built there some of the handsome homes that adorn the
city, and which they occupy usually for a few months
each year. Their social functions are attended with
much magnificence, and they have the *entrée* to official
society, and frequently to that exclusive circle of aristo-
cratic old families, many of whom have lived there in
unostentatious elegance ever since the nation transferred
its capital to the banks of the Potomac.

For a time Mary Leiter attended the school in
Washington founded some years ago by Madam
Burr and subsequently conducted by her daughters.
She was a good student. Quiet in her manner, she
emitted only occasionally that sparkle of wit or fun
that so often flashes from the happy school girl of

fourteen. She exercised, however, a fascination to which both her teachers and companions were susceptible. Her beauty of face, her pose and carriage, together with a sweet, girlish modesty and a graciousness that was simple and unaffected, rendered her at all times most attractive.

The greater part of Miss Leiter's education, however, was conducted at home, under governesses, and her individual tastes and talents thus developed. Travel, and a more or less prolonged residence abroad at various times under most happy circumstances, cultivated her powers of observation and developed in her that breadth of mental vision that at an unusually early period not only removed the crudities of youth, but gave her that poise and finish that made her so charming to men and women of mature and brilliant intellect.

Comparatively little was heard of her family socially till after her *début*, which occurred in the winter of 1888, and their present social prominence in the United States is due to the remarkable impression she everywhere created. As a new-comer she was viewed critically, for she aimed always at the highest and best in the social castes of her country. She was weighed in the balance with the daughters of better known and longer established families of the East, and was found their equal in beauty and breeding and frequently their peer in charm of manner and intellect.

In Washington her father leased the home, on Dupont Circle, of the late James G. Blaine, and there Miss Leiter spent the first years of her young womanhood, during which such homage was paid her that she never entered a drawing-room nor crossed a ball-room without attracting the attention and gaze of every one. She planned and directed the numerous social functions given there by her parents on a scale of magnificence that was not easily approached, and she brought to the house a fame such as it never derived from the occupancy of its distinguished owner nor any of his family.

When her father built his own home, which is considered by many people the most beautiful in Washington, her taste found a new field for its display, both in the plan of its construction and in its final decorations. It was minutely described in the press of the country, particular emphasis being given to the apartments appropriated to Miss Leiter's use, so undoubtedly was she the social genius of her family and the figure who held the interest of the public.

A few years ago the favorable verdict of a man whom a recent historian of New York society has designated its self-appointed dictator went far towards establishing a woman's reputation for beauty or distinction on a national footing. Mr. Ward McAllister undoubtedly wielded a singular power and influence, and his unqualified admiration of Miss Leiter, while it reflects to-day much credit upon his judgment, played at the time a considerable part in the wide spread of her fame.

Her development was rapid and continuous, and she rose in the course of a few years to a national prominence. It has been said of her that she was not true to early friendships. " The law of nature is alteration forevermore," and every mind that expands must outgrow the objects that satisfied it at one period of its existence unless they are capable in a degree of keeping pace with its progress. As a matter of fact, while there was a graciousness in her manner towards all with whom she came in contact, she formed but few close friendships, the natural reserve of her temperament rendering it impossible for her to respond easily to those intimacies which enter into the lives of so many girls.

During the second administration of President Cleveland there existed between his young wife and Miss Leiter a degree of friendship that was as flattering to one as it was to the other, for the Clevelands enjoyed the reputation of choosing their friends for their personal charm.

During both of his terms of office Mr. Cleveland had a home in the suburbs of Washington, where he and his family passed much time between seasons, and where they frequently entertained the friends whom they admitted more or less to their intimacy. There, during the spring of the year in which she was married, Miss Leiter passed every Sunday prior to that event, carrying away with her to another land a vivid impression of one of the most admirable women who ever adorned public life in America.

England was by no means an unknown country to Miss Leiter. She had been accustomed from her early childhood to spending much time in Europe, and a London season, which is the climax of many an American girl's social ambition, was not a new experience to her. The season of 1894, however, marked a turning-point in her life. Hon. Thomas F. Bayard, who was our Ambassador at the Court of St. James at the time, had been married not long before to Miss May Clymer, of Washington, a daughter of Dr. Clymer, of the navy, and a granddaughter of Admiral Shubrick. The Bayards had known Miss Leiter at home, and they undoubtedly contributed much to the reception she everywhere met during that season in England, for they themselves were much sought after, and the distinction of their position gave prominence to her. They brought her into contact with a class of men and women among whom her own highly endowed mind found an inspiration on whose wings she rose in a short time to a new fame.

Among those who paid her the tribute of a profound admiration was a rising young secretary of the kingdom, a man of scholarly tastes and an author of established reputation.

"I found," recently wrote Julian Ralph from India, "a sure key to the viceroy's character in between the lines of a dozen speeches that he made in January and February, 1899. Some of his qualities, more especially his quick sympathy, humor, and the sentimental and romantic inclination, are rather more American than English. . . . It is consoling to us Americans to find that the man who has attracted so much beauty and talent away from our country is himself the next thing to an American."

When he met Miss Leiter, though he was but thirty-five years of age, Mr. Curzon had been a member of Parliament, representing the district of Southport, for eight years. He had already wealth and distinction, and was the heir to the title of his father, who is the fourth Baron Scarsdale. His ambition, moreover, was of that high order which found in Miss Leiter a responsive attitude and a quickening sympathy. His literary and political career—in a word, the position he had made for himself through his own talents—was to her a matter of far deeper interest than the eventual inheritance of his father's estate and title. The reputation which his writings on the political questions in the East had given him particularly attracted her admiration.

Replying four years later to the address of welcome delivered to him by the city of Bombay, Lord Curzon expressed gratification at its kindly tone both for himself and his wife, who, he said, came to India with sympathies as warm as his own, and who looked forward with earnest delight to a life of happy labor in the midst of its people.

The interest which Miss Leiter's remarkable career had inspired intensified with the announcement of her approaching marriage. Her home was besieged by newspaper correspondents representing all sections of the country, showing how widely she was known.

The 22d of April—the date selected for her wedding

Mattie Mitchell
(Duchesse de Rochefoucauld)
From photograph by C. M. Bell

—was an ideal spring day. At an early hour in the morning people began to gather around St. John's Episcopal Church in Washington, where the ceremony was to be performed at half-past eleven o'clock, with a hope of catching a glimpse of the fair and famous bride. By eleven o'clock the streets and sidewalks and Lafayette Square were solidly banked with spectators, and it was with difficulty that a passage-way was kept open for the carriages of those who had been invited to witness the ceremony. Women cried out that they were being crushed, and others fainted, yet the crowd continued to increase till the moment of the bride's arrival.

St. John's Church, one of the oldest in Washington, is constructed without a central aisle, so that bridal parties enter by one side aisle and return by the other. Thither have wended their way many couples that have passed into fame and history. At its altar, a little more than six years before Miss Leiter pronounced her marriage vows, another American girl, Miss Mary Endicott, of Massachusetts, whose father was at the time Secretary of War, gave her hand to a distinguished son of Great Britain, Hon. Joseph Chamberlain.

The ceremonies at both of these marriages were exquisitely simple. Bishop Talbott, of Wyoming, officiated at that of Miss Leiter and Mr. Curzon, assisted by Rev. Dr. Mackay Smith, the pastor of the church. Lord Lamington acted as best man for Mr. Curzon, and Miss Leiter was attended by her two sisters. She was singularly pale, and, enveloped in the whiteness of her bridal veil and gown, the Easter lilies that adorned the altar and chancel seemed not more fair than she. Her slender figure looked its full height, which is the same as her father's,—five feet seven inches. Her face, whose every feature is indicative of character and perhaps too serious when in repose, but wholly charming when lighted by a smile which expresses so much intelligence and sympathy, bore evidence of the recollection of her thoughts. It was, as it is to-day, a face of unusual beauty, oval in shape, with dark-gray eyes, straight black brows, a sweet, sensitive mouth, a prettily shaped nose, and a low forehead with fine black hair brushed simply away from it and emphasizing its whiteness.

On her wedding-day she solved with her usual good sense a problem that has confronted many brides since gloves first came to be considered a requisite of their costume, as to how under such circumstances a ring may be gracefully assumed. She entered and left the church with hands uncovered and unadorned save by her engagement-ring with its superb setting, a ruby and two diamonds, and the gold band which supplemented it.

The ceremony was witnessed by Mrs. Cleveland, the Cabinet Ministers and their families, the diplomatic corps, and a number of people of purely social prominence from several cities in the United States and England.

For the reception which followed, the bride's beautiful home was decorated entirely with peach-, cherry-, and apple-blossoms. She stood beneath her own portrait, whose frame was suggestively outlined with forget-me-nots, to receive the many who gathered about her with good wishes and good-byes.

The first days of her honeymoon were spent at "Beauvoir," the suburban Washington home of Mr. and Mrs. John R. McLean, who placed it at her disposal for that period. There she entertained several times at dinner, that Mr. Curzon might meet some of the people who give charm to the society of the American capital.

The year of his marriage proved also an eventful one in the public life of Mr. Curzon. He was made Under Secretary of State for Foreign Affairs and Privy Councillor, and re-elected to his seat in Parliament, all within that brief period.

Shortly after Mr. Curzon's return to England the fall of the Rosebery cabinet necessitated a new Parliamentary election. His American bride entered into the English political campaign of the summer of 1895 with an enthusiasm that was the delight of his constituents and the admiration of his opponents. It was a first test of her power in a field that called forth her best efforts, and as she became conscious of her strength and of the possibility of being a force in the political life of a great country, the highest attributes of her nature unfolded themselves. Among a people who "make a romance of marriage," an electioneering tour before the honeymoon had waned roused an interest upon whose results no politician, however astute, could reckon. Not only did Mrs. Curzon accompany her husband on the occasions when he addressed the people of his borough, but, quite independent of him, she drove through the Southport district of Lancashire, seeing the wives of his constituents and even the electors themselves, and manifesting an intelligent interest in the political affairs of their country that, from a foreigner and a beautiful young woman, conveyed a most delicate flattery and subtle gratification.

A Liberal paper, commenting on the election after the vote had been cast, gallantly insisted that Curzon owed his success far more to the winning smiles and irresistible charm of his American wife than he did to his own speeches.

The following four years of Lady Curzon's life were spent in England between a town house in London and her husband's country-seat, Kedleston Hall, in Derbyshire. Two daughters were born to her within that period, the first in 1896 and the younger in August, 1898, shortly after Mr. Curzon's appointment to the Governor-Generalship of India.

Mrs. Curzon's parents visited her every summer, and her father bought for her the London residence, Number One Carlton House Terrace, the first in a row of twenty-two handsome houses with a colonnade of marble pillars, overlooking St. James Park, one of the most exclusive localities in London.

In close companionship and absolute sympathy with a statesman whose life promised greatness, in the full enjoyment of a social existence in which the grace and strength of her personality had already made them-

Mary Victoria Leiter
(Baroness Curzon of Kedleston)
From photograph by Miss Alice Hughes

selves felt, happily placed in all her relations to life, it would have seemed, in consideration of the youth of both herself and her husband, that for the time being at least their measure of good fortune was well filled. In the summer of 1898, however, Mr. Curzon was offered the greatest gift of the British government, the Governor-Generalship of India. Until Mr. Balfour's authoritative announcement of the fact in the House of Commons many people had discredited the rumor on the ground that such an office had never been offered to a Commoner.

In India, which Mr. Curzon had visited frequently and where he had already become thoroughly known through his writings, the news of his nomination was received with entire satisfaction. In London it excited unusual interest.

In addition to more or less lengthy editorial comment, every journal reviewed his strikingly brilliant career, and in enumerating his unusual advantages through which he might hope for success in the discharge of the duties of the high office he had accepted, his American wife was ranked among the first. It was regarded as a happy circumstance that such a woman should partake of the glories and responsibilities of his position.

According to an old English statute, a man who is duly elected to the House of Commons may not resign his seat. It may be vacated only by death, expulsion, legal disqualifications, or by accepting an office from the crown. As soon as Mr. Curzon was nominated to succeed Lord Elgin, whose term as Governor-General of India still had several months to run, in order to enable him to sever his connection with the Parliament, he received from the queen the appointment of High Steward and Bailiff of the Manor of Northstead.

The office, however, is merely honorary, and was retained only until he was officially proclaimed governor-general. His seat in Parliament at the election following his withdrawal was carried by the Liberal candidate, the late Sir Herbert Naylor Leyland, whose wife, another beautiful American, Miss Jennie Chamberlain, of Cleveland, had played much the same part in his campaign as Mrs. Curzon, under similar circumstances, had taken in that of her husband.

During the month following Mr. Curzon's appointment to the governor-generalship he was elevated to the peerage as Baron Curzon of Kedleston. As the name in which he had made his reputation, he desired to retain Curzon in his title.

The eldest son of Earl Howe being Viscount Curzon, however, he was obliged to agree to two conditions imposed by Lord Howe,—first, to be known now as Curzon of Kedleston, and, second, on succeeding to his father's title, to drop Curzon Kedleston, which was never to be resumed either by himself or his heirs.

A new life, quite unlike anything she had known, now opened before Lady Curzon,—a life of real power over millions of subjects, a life of significant ceremonial and regal pomp, in which this daughter of a republic assumed with her husband the leading *rôle*.

She entered completely into its spirit, planning all the details of a sumptuous existence which is so highly gratifying to an Eastern people and in such perfect accord with its conceptions of power. India likes to see the outward form of empire, and measures thereby its internal strength.

Lady Curzon was already familiar with the political and historical side of the country whither fortune was leading her. For her acquaintance with its social side, which more especially concerned her, she equipped herself with that same faultless taste that had marked her career in the society of her own country and England.

With the lavish hospitality she had in contemplation, she ordered, several weeks before her departure from England, thousands of cards of invitation for dinners, evening receptions, and garden-parties, including menu cards and ball programmes. For all of these occasions she provided herself with the appropriate habiliments whose exquisite details, the art with which they were chosen, and the genius with which they were worn, becoming identified with her personal beauty, acquired shortly after her appearance in Calcutta a fame as wide as the empire.

Her last days in England forshadowed the glories of her life in India. At a ball given at Welbeck Abbey by the Duke and Duchess of Portland in honor of the Duke and Duchess of Connaught, shortly before her departure, Lady Curzon of Kedleston, whose grace had once given charm to many an American ball-room, was among the few honored with a place in the royal quadrille. While the Portlands do not entertain often, they enjoy the reputation of having the most sumptuous social functions that are witnessed anywhere in England. Their supper-tables glitter with a gold service of great artistic and intrinsic value, and their spacious picture-gallery makes a ball-room whose attractiveness is seldom rivalled.

For several days Lord and Lady Curzon were guests at Welbeck, going from there to Southport to make a farewell visit to Lord Curzon's old Parliamentary district, in which Lady Curzon had won votes and admiration in the first days of her residence in England. The locomotive of the train in which they made the journey was decorated with the royal standard and the stars-and-stripes, Lady Curzon's nationality being, as it always is, thus gracefully remembered. The streets of the town were similarly decorated, including, besides the insignia of the two great Anglo-Saxon countries, the star of India.

It was a memorable day in Southport, whose population turned out *en masse* to welcome them, the city and county functionaries in their official robes greeting them at the railroad station. As they drove through the streets of the town, their coach drawn by four horses, the bells of Christ Church peeled forth a joyous welcome, and pride and admiration shone in every face that lined the route to the art-gallery. There they held a public reception, Sir William Forwood presiding and making a speech, in which he dwelt with gratification upon the unqualified approval expressed by the nation at Lord Curzon's appointment as Governor-General of India, and referred gallantly to the charm which the young American vicereine would impart to the court.

On the 30th of December Lord and Lady Curzon landed at Bombay amid the firing of a royal salute from the war-ships in port. The city welcomed them with a display of much magnificence in its decorations and a manifestation of genuine cordiality, presenting its address to that effect in an elaborately wrought silver casket.

At the governor's house they were received by Lord and Lady Sandhurst, Lord Sandhurst being Governor of Bombay, and ranking second in authority to the governor-general.

It was here that Lord and Lady Curzon made their first social appearance in India at a ball and reception given in their honor. Beyond the fact that Lord Curzon's wife was an American, prior to that night India knew but little of her. Happy and beautiful, with the added brilliancy which appreciation and success impart to every woman, she made instantly an impression of loveliness which in a few days had spread over India and still prevails,—resting now, however, on a more enduring basis.

The impression, in fact, created by both Lord and Lady Curzon at Bombay paved the way to the enthusiasm with which they were received at Calcutta a few days later.

The city was richly decorated, the American flag being everywhere conspicuously displayed amid evidences of Oriental splendor. It has been estimated that not less than one hundred thousand people witnessed the magnificent spectacle of their reception at the palace.

The imposing width of the double terrace of steps that lead to the main entrance was covered with a rich red carpet terminating in the green sward of the lawn, where, in the magnificent uniform of the army forming part of the military service of India, one hundred men of the Calcutta Rifles and one hundred men of the First Gloucester Regiment, in scarlet, with their band, stood attention.

At the foot of the steps the Life-Guard, in gorgeous red array, consisting of one hundred and twenty Indians selected for their fine size and physique, grouped itself. At the top, two colossal palms lifted their noble branches, while the vine-clad balustrades added another touch of color to the picturesque setting of the scene, which was further enhanced by the presence of many native chiefs and dignitaries in the splendor of their rich attire.

In the distance the cannon of Fort Williams boomed a mighty welcome to the new powers as they drove under the great arch of the outer gate surmounted by its massive lions. Beneath the limitless blue of a tropical sky, with everywhere the luxuriant verdure of a tropical landscape, this was the scene, reflecting both the power of England and the magnificence and antiquity of the Orient, that greeted Lady Curzon, who had opened her eyes on life thirty years before in a new city of a new world thousands of miles away.

To the vast concourse of Europeans and Orientals who beheld Lord and Lady Curzon as they mounted the steps and entered the palace they conveyed a sense of entire satisfaction, so absolutely do they realize in stature, bearing, and poise the conception of a noble sovereignty. Lord Curzon is more than six feet in height and of proportionate breadth, while his whole manner denotes the vigor of youth, mentally as well as physically.

It is a strange coincidence, first, that the Government House at Calcutta should have been built by the Marquis of Wellesley, who at a later period, during his Governor-Generalship of Ireland, married, as already stated, the beautiful Baltimorean, Mary Caton Patterson, and, in the second place, that it should have been copied, with slight modification, from Lord Curzon's ancestral home, Kedleston Hall. After a visit to the latter place, Wellesley declared that if he ever had a house to build he should take it for his model.

In 1799, during his term as Governor-General of India, it fell to his lot to erect at Calcutta the viceregal palace known as Government House, and he built it on a plan well in keeping with the dignity of the great European power which rules over two-thirds of India.

The first two social events held at Government House after the instalment of Lord Curzon as governor-general were the levee on the 7th of January,

1899, which was attended by sixteen hundred gentlemen, and the drawing-room on the 12th of the same month, at which Lady Curzon wore her viceregal honors with irresistible graciousness. After the presentations, which were made in the throne-room, Lord and Lady Curzon standing in front of the magnificent gold throne upon a velvet-covered dais, she went up into the ball-room, which occupies the entire third floor of the central portion of the palace, and which is said to be one of the handsomest in the world, and there mingled among her guests with a grace as charming and unaffected as if she were again hostess in either her American or her English home instead of the representative of the Queen of England and Empress of India.

When we consider her exalted position and her unusual personality, the rapidity with which she has established herself in the affections of the people all over the empire ceases to be a matter of wonderment. The good judgment and tact of both the viceroy and his wife have prevented them from falling into the grave error of some of their predecessors in showing a preference for the European over the educated native element. As a result, Lady Curzon's praises have been proclaimed by the latter in the glowing language that is peculiar to them as frequently as they have been by the former. Ram Sharma, an Indian poet, referred to her, in the course of some lines of welcome addressed to Lord Curzon, as

" A rose of roses bright,
A vision of embodied light."

Miss May Handy
From photograph by James L. Breese

Another native scribe, when she received the decoration of the Imperial Order of the Crown of India, declared her to be "like a diamond set in gold, or the full moon in a clear autumnal sky."

Not only by her youth and beauty and her social graces, however, has she endeared herself to the people of India. With a high appreciation of the viceregal position and of the duty owing to their subjects under all circumstances, Lord and Lady Curzon last winter made a tour of the plague-stricken districts of the empire. Besides advising and making intelligent suggestions to those who were working among the sufferers, they in many cases personally provided for their care, and by unselfish heroism bound the whole nation to them by ties of profound gratitude and a tender personal affection, augmenting thereby India's loyalty to the queen-empress.

The wives and families of India's viceroys have found a broad field for the exercise of their benevolent tendencies, and not a few have left here noble monuments to the memory of their days in the great black empire. Eden Gardens is one, the beautiful public park adjoining the grounds of the viceregal residence and the gift of Lord Auckland's sisters to the city of Calcutta. The Dufferin Medical Mission is another, inaugurated by Lady Dufferin during the governor-generalship of her husband as a means of providing medical help for the women of India.

A few weeks after her arrival in the empire Lady Curzon presided at a meeting of the central committee of the Dufferin fund, and manifested a keen interest in the noble charity.

It has within the last thirty years become customary for the entire English government in India to spend the six hot months of the year in Simla, the town in the Himalayan hills whose singular natural and social topography have become familiar in late years to many English readers through Kipling's Indian tales. The Foreign Office at London recently expended a large sum of money in the erection of suitable buildings there, including a new viceregal residence that is a vast improvement over its predecessor, which was little more than a cottage. It was perched on a precipitous crag, and Lady Dufferin used to compare it to the ark balanced on Mount Ararat, adding that in the rainy season she herself felt like Mrs. Noah.

The villa at Simla and the palaces at Calcutta and at Barrackpore on the river near the capital constitute the trio of viceregal residences in which the Curzons are passing the five years of their life in India. None of them is a home in the meaning we give that word,— a place of privacy and relaxation,—for each has its own degree of state and formality. They live to-day in the glare of the world, with no more seclusion than ever falls either to "the head that wears a crown" or to those to whom it delegates its power. The state that encompasses them does not conceal the personality of either, and both are full of interest.

Marrying a man whose life promised so much, Mary Leiter has undoubtedly been a factor in the early culmination of that promise. She is spoken of through-out India with love and pride, and when Lord Curzon's day comes to pass the government into other hands, it may be that the empire will be placarded with signs, as it was, says a recent historian, when Lord Ripon retired, bearing a legend similar to that they bore then: "We want more Curzons!"

NEW YORK AS A SOCIAL CENTRE

THE women who, both at home and abroad, are regarded as the leaders of American society in these last days of the century are or have been, almost without exception, at some time in their career identified with New York. Though there is no city in the United States that fills the central position which Paris holds in reference to all France, and which London occupies, at least socially, in England, the geographical position of New York, to a nation whose progressive spirit inspires it with a keen interest in the doings of the entire world, has given it a leading place, and to the commanding position it holds in the financial life of the American people it undoubtedly owes much of its prominence as a social centre.

Those who at present constitute its ruling element, and who in the eyes of the country at large form the unit of New York society, are, as a rule, the possessors of enormous wealth. The elegance of their various homes, the magnificence of their hospitalities, the luxurious state in which they travel, all tend to give them an immense influence in a young country where such a princely scale of existence was practically unknown thirty-five years ago, and where there are many striving for similar results.

Catherine Duer
(Mrs. Clarence Mackay)

NEW YORK AS A SOCIAL CENTRE

Women born of this class, and who possess, in addition to the advantages it bestows upon them, personal gifts of an unusual order, have from the very outset of their social career a remarkable fame and prestige. In some instances they come of families who have been distinguished in the life of New York since the days when the homes of the people who made up its one set were gathered about the battery and lower end of the town, and when the division of its classes was the natural one of condition, and not the arbitrary one which its abnormal growth has entailed upon it in recent years.

New York's belles in the early century were for the most part native, and anything so remote as the Pacific coast, whence comes one of its belles of the present era, entered nobody's wildest dreams.

A Franklin flies his kite, a Fulton is born, a Morse flashes his reverent thought fifty miles in the twinkling of an eye, and lo! the ages in which man crept and groped have rolled from us. Distance has lost the meaning it had a little more than a hundred years ago, when Lady Kitty Duer was accounted one of the belles of New York; they come now from every section of the country to add their charm to the life of the metropolis.

Many of these beautiful women, moreover, are as celebrated in European capitals as they are throughout America, and it is difficult to estimate how much of our fame in the eyes of other nations we owe to them. To stand forth, however, in their own country as beings unusually gifted is quite as great a triumph to-day as it was more than a hundred years ago.

"Your countrywoman, Mrs. Wolcott," said the minister from England, admiring the beauty of the Connecticut statesman's wife, to an official of the young government in the days when its capital was located in New York, "would be admired even at St. James."

"Sir," replied the American, "she is admired even on Litchfield Hill."

INDEX

A

Adams, Hannah, 150
Adams, John, 22
Adams, John Quincy, 74
Adams, Mrs. John, 14
Alabama, story of, 105
Albany, Duke of, 202
Allen, James Lane, 148
Alston, Joseph, 30, 38
Alston, Mrs. Joseph. See Theodosia
  Burr
American Graces, 62, 66
Amory, William, 97
André, Major, 191
Ariosto, 116
Armstrong, General, 50
Armstrong, Vene P., 159
Astor, Mrs., 111
Atlantic Transport Company, 255
August, Tom, 179
Ayot, Alexis, 145

B

Bache, Mrs. Richard, 193
Bache, Richard, 193
Baily, Dr. Gamaliel, 214
Baker, Mrs. George W., 171
Baltimore, city of, 39
Bard, Dr., 29
Barney, Commodore, 44
Barton, Dr. Benjamin, 87
Barton, Mrs. Thomas Pennant. See
  Cora Livingston
Barton, Thomas Pennant, 87
Bateman, Abraham, 254
Bayard, Hon. Thomas F., 271
Beaconsfield, Lord, 248

Beale, General, 88
Beauregard, General, 234
" Beauvoir," 275
Bellefontaine Cemetery, 263
Bentham, Jeremy, 19
Benton, Jessie, 123
Benton, Thomas Hart, 123, 125, 126
Bernhardt, Sarah, 200
Bingham, Mrs. William, 192
Bingham, William, 192
Bladensburg duel, 85
Blaine, James G., 268
Blenheim Palace, 244
Blennerhassett, 34
Bodisco, Baron, 127
Bolin, Lieutenant-Governor, 92
Bonaparte, Jerome, 28, 43, 44, 64
Bonaparte, Jerome Napoleon, 53, 59
Bonaparte, Louis Napoleon, 59
Bonaparte, Madame Jerome, 39, 67.
  See Elizabeth Patterson
Bonaparte, Napoleon, 42, 43, 48, 51,
  55, 67
Bonaparte, Pauline, 56, 58
Bonsteller, Baron, 57
Borghese, Princess. See Pauline
  Bonaparte
Boston Library, 88
Bourne, Sylvanus, 53
Bradley-Martin, Mrs., 255
Brant, Indian Chief, 29
Brattle, Thomas, 92
Bremer, Frederika, 108, 115
Bright, Mr. John, 247
British Society, 239
Browning, Mrs., 114
Buchanan, James, 161, 164, 167, 170,
  174 181, 232

291

INDEX

INDEX

INDEX

INDEX

INDEX

INDEX

THE END